when your child has a...

Strong-Willed Personality

✓ Understand Your Child's Needs

✓ Tailor Your Parenting Techniques

✓ Help Your Child Adapt

Carl Pickhardt

Series Editor: Vincent Iannelli, M.D.

Aadamsmedia

Avon, Massachusetts

Published by
Adams Media, an F+W Publications Company
57 Littlefield Street, Avon, MA 02322. U.S.A.
www.adamsmedia.com

Contains materials adapted and abridged from *The Everything® Parent's
Guide to the Strong-Willed Child*, by Carl Pickhardt, copyright © 2005
by F+W Publications, Inc., ISBN 13: 978-1-59337-381-8, ISBN 10:
1-59337-381-3.

ISBN 13: 978-1-59869-763-6
ISBN 10: 1-59869-763-3

Printed in Canada.

J I H G F E D C B A

Library of Congress Cataloging-in-Publication Data
is available from the publisher.

This publication is designed to provide accurate and authoritative
information with regard to the subject matter covered. It is sold with
the understanding that the publisher is not engaged in rendering legal,
accounting, or other professional advice. If legal advice or other expert
assistance is required, the services of a competent professional person
should be sought.

—From a *Declaration of Principles* jointly adopted by
a Committee of the American Bar Association
and a Committee of Publishers and Associations

Many of the designations used by manufacturers and sellers to distinguish
their product are claimed as trademarks. Where those designations appear in
this book and Adams Media was aware of a trademark claim, the designations
have been printed with initial capital letters.

*This book is available at quantity discounts for bulk purchases.
For information, please call 1-800-289-0963.*

Contents

Chapter 4: *Adapting and Cooperating—Methods for Parenting...59*

Chapter 5: *Who's Running Your Family?...79*

Chapter 6: *How to Get Back in Charge...93*

Chapter 7: *Bumps on the Road to Regaining Control...111*

Introduction

by Vincent Iannelli

Although parents often seek help when they have a picky eater or poor sleeper, they often try to go it alone when their child has discipline and behavior problems.

They may stick to their own previously tried and true discipline techniques or go from one "breakthrough" program to another, without any success.

Unfortunately, while many kids are easy to discipline, eager to please, and sometimes do well even as you make parenting mistakes, with the strong-willed child you have to be more flexible and adapt your method of parenting to your child.

This can be quite surprising to the new parents who read about all of the traditional parenting techniques and thought they were prepared to their raise their child. Parents who already have one or more easygoing children and then have a strong-willed child come along can be in for an even bigger surprise as they continue to try the discipline methods that worked with their first children but no longer seem to be working anymore.

Their initial surprise quickly leads to frustration, as their strong-willed child almost seems to take over the family. His tantrums and demands may get so bad that it makes eating out at a restaurant, going to a store, or even visiting family or friends a big chore.

It is at this point, but hopefully before, that parents seek help. *When Your Child Has a . . . Strong-Willed Personality* is a great resource for parents who need help parenting their strong-willed child.

In addition to helping you understand why your child may be so strong-willed, Dr. Pickhardt shows you how to get back in charge of your household. His book teaches you how to handle discipline, conflict, and how to avoid overreacting when your strong-willed child doesn't listen.

From the basics of what to say during a tantrum and how to help your child work in a group of children to teaching your child to be more patient, *When Your Child Has a . . . Strong-Willed Personality* will give you all of the tools you need to parent your strong-willed child.

While it is the perfect book for strong-willed children and other hard-to-discipline children, including kids with ADHD, it is also a great resource for any parent who wants to learn more about basic discipline techniques and avoid overparenting.

Chapter 1

Is Your Child Strong-Willed?

Ten Things You Will Learn in This Chapter

- How to tell if your infant may be a willful child.

- When children start to act out, purposefully, and why.

- What happens when a stubborn child and stubborn parent clash.

- How following through on your word is extremely important.

- About the four propositions of independence.

- How distraction can be a valuable tool.

- About the hidden meaning behind the question "why?"

- How a willful child often only gets worse with age.

- How to deal with your child who demands immediate gratification.

- About first-born children and their interesting perspectives of family

The Issue of Want

To begin to appreciate how willful children can be a handful for parents, it may be helpful to consider the six Ws of willfulness—want, won't, why, win, when, and whose. Around each of these issues, parents of a willful child frequently find themselves hard-pressed.

Although most parents know the basics of what their baby requires—food, rest, diaper changes, comforting, playtime, sleep, soothing words, affectionate touch, for example—only the baby knows exactly when he wants those needs met. Some babies are flexible, easily scheduled, and soon satisfied, quickly coming to adjust to the timing, kind, and amount of parental care being given. Living on parental terms seems to work okay for the child because, by and large, the child goes with the parental program without complaining.

Other babies, however, are less content with this standard schedule. Operating on their own schedule, they loudly let it be known when a want is unsatisfied, and they signal intense and protracted distress until it is met. They also signal to parents that a strong-willed child has arrived into their care. "She just keeps fussing and crying until we give her what she wants. She won't give up!" In willful children, where there's a will, there's a want.

Now parents wonder, "Maybe we shouldn't respond to every cry if the more often she complains, the more often we give her what she wants. After all, we don't want to spoil her. Besides, she's supposed to live on our terms. We're not supposed to live on hers." So the parents decide to let the infant cry herself down after they have already settled her in bed three times, and after half an hour of wailing, the exhausted child finally does give in to sleep. "Now she's learned who's in charge," conclude the parents, "although it sure is hard hearing her be that unhappy for that long."

DOES THIS SOUND LIKE YOUR CHILD?

Because willful children are so strongly wed to what they want, they will often be impulsively short-sighted, focusing on immediate desire instead of long-term interest. It is the parent's job to extend the willful child's vision, to think ahead about possible costs and risks, to delay what is wanted and consider what is right and wise.

But this is usually a mistake. For the baby to feel firmly bonded to parents, to feel empowered to express a want and know that it will be met, and to predict that parental care is there when needed, parents need to meet the baby's needs any time the infant has the will to express an identifiable want. During the first year of life, rewarding a willful want with the desired response is not spoiling the infant; it is helping that hungry, lonely, hurting, or frightened little child to feel attached, secure, trustful, confident, and effective.

The Issue of Won't
By age two, most children normally begin opposing parental rules and requests by delaying or refusing to do what they are told to do or not to do. This obstinacy is

an act of courage—the child's daring to resist the most powerful people in her world. Appearing to test adult authority, the child is really testing her growing power of personal choice.

In most cases, if parents continue to be firm and insistent in their request and don't overreact and fuel the child's refusal by getting upset, the boy or girl learns to go along with what parents want most of the time. The willful child, however, is more intense and more dedicated to refusal, often surprising parents at the way he digs in his heels and makes a scene when he decides not to do what they ask and they continue to insist. In willful children, where there's a will, there's a won't.

Beware similarity conflicts between stubborn parent and stubborn child, each refusing to give in to the other or back down. The harder the parent refuses, the harder the child learns to refuse in return. Better for the parent to disengage and think of another, less confrontational approach to take—like talking out and working out the conflict instead of stubbornly going toe to toe.

"Won't" Can Wear a Parent Down

It is the intensity and persistence of the willful child's "won't" that wears parents down, sometimes causing them to relent. And when they relent, the child feels more empowered. Parents may get too tired to keep after the request they made after the child delays or refuses, or they may feel uncomfortable in conflict, and so they back off. And when they do, the child learns that delay and refusal work. For parents, the lesson is simple: Don't request what you are not prepared to pursue to fulfillment. Mean what you say. Carry through with what you say you want.

A willful "won't" can also take other common forms. The willful child often won't admit making a mistake, won't admit having done something wrong, won't apologize for doing wrong, and won't accept constructive criticism for mistakes or correction for misbehavior. "Leave me alone! I don't want to listen to you! I don't want to talk about it!" But parents must be steadfast: "You can put off the discussion, but you cannot make it go away. Before you get to do anything else you want to do, we will need to have our talk."

Four Propositions for Independence

At a very young age, a willful child can come to four very significant understandings about parental influence: the four propositions for independence. These propositions are:

- "My parents won't always stick to what they say."
- "My parents can't make me."
- "My parents can't stop me."
- "My choices are up to me."

Each successful "won't" only encourages the child to feel more confident in his or her power of resistance. Of course, understanding these four propositions for independence is empowering at any age, but the willful child tends to learn them very young. Then, when parents punish refusal, the willful child loses the skirmish, but wins the battle. Punishment just certifies the child's power to disobey. It is better for parents to let the child know that disobedience is a choice the child is free to make, but not a choice parents are willing to live with. "You can choose to delay what we want, but you can't get out of doing what we want, because we will keep after you and after you until it gets done. And before you get anything else you want from us, we will get what we want from you."

A BETTER PARENTING PRACTICE

When a child under the age of three refuses what you ask with a "won't," use distraction and then return to pursue what you are after. Distract the child from the negative situation into doing something positive with you (thus breaking the child's negative mindset) and then, after a few minutes of pleasure or play, return to your original request. Repeat this procedure as often as necessary to gain the child's consent.

Try This Method—Distract-and-Return

So how are parents to deal with a willful "won't" at the tender ages of one to three? Distract-and-return is best. Instead of arguing with your child or insisting that he do what you want when he refuses, distract the child to something positive. "Come look at this." "Come play with me for a minute." Then, having restored a positive context to the relationship, return to your original request in a few minutes and see if your child is not more inclined to cooperate. If so, reward his compliance with approval, appreciation, affection, or praise. If he is not yet in a mood to comply, distract the child again and draw his attention to something else positive and then return to your request again. In general, parents have more power to be consistent with what they want than the child has power to consistently maintain a stubborn "won't," particularly when the parent keeps disrupting the child's stubborn refusal with positive distract-and-return methods.

But suppose your willful child has caught you in a time crunch. He refuses to put on his shoes so you can leave to pick his brother up on time when the school bus arrives. Now you have to weigh which is more important—a timely pick up of your older child or an obediently shod younger child before you leave. In order not to penalize the older for the younger, you take the younger barefoot. You win some, and you lose some. However, what you lose on today you resolve to start working on earlier tomorrow. And you're even prepared to bargain his "want" for your "will." "If you *want* to have your usual snack with your brother when he gets home from school tomorrow, you *will* need to have your shoes on when we leave to pick him up."

The Issue of Why

Now consider the preadolescent eight-year-old, feeling grown up enough in childhood to question parental rules and restraints to want an explanation. "Why should I? I want to know why," the child asks. So parents take the child seriously and take the time to explain, and the curious child, feeling satisfied, complies.

With a willful child, however, "Why?" is not simply a request for information, it is a challenge to parental authority. Roughly translated, it complains, "I shouldn't have to!" At issue is what right parents have to tell the willful child what to do or not to do. It's not information the child is after; it's justification. In willful children, where there's a will, there's a why.

DID YOU KNOW?

Parenting is not a popularity contest. A strong-willed child may often see your rules as simply there to frustrate his wants. You must explain that it is not for pleasure or power that you take these stands but for a purpose—to protect and promote his best interests.

The Meaning of Why

The problem is, when parents give an explanation for their demand or limit, the willful child protests, "That's not a good reason!" And with such a child, there never is a reason good enough to justify being asked to do something she doesn't want to do or being denied something she wants.

Willful children also frequently ask "why?" because they feel entitled to know more than parents may want to tell. "Why we won't buy what you want is because we're trying to spend less right now as a family," explain the parents, not wanting to go into details about one partner's possibility of being laid off at work. But with willful children, one "why?" just seems to beget another. "Why do we need to spend less now?"

The Parent Rules

To the "Why?" requesting an explanation that parents either cannot or do not want to give, it is best to stop the endless questioning by simply saying (and repeating if necessary), "This is what we can tell you; we cannot tell you any more."

To the "Why?" that challenges their right to authority, parents can repeatedly explain something else: how they are obliged to follow "the parent rules" (of responsible parenting), even when that obedience is hard to do. "The reason why we have the right to tell you what you can and cannot do is because your welfare is our responsibility. So long as you depend on us, the parent rules say that we must set rules and limits for you. The hardest part of our job is doing what we feel is right when you feel we are wrong. But because we love you, we will do the best job for you we can, even when you don't agree with what we are doing. Just remember: we are never against you when we oppose what you want. We are on your side, out to help you, not hurt you. And it gives us no pleasure to act for you in ways you do not like."

The Issue of Win

Come early adolescence, between ages nine and thirteen, the child typically begins the separation from childhood and no longer wants to be defined and treated as "just a child" anymore.

Now there is more opposition to parents from a young person who increasingly doesn't like being told what she can and cannot do. Pushing against and away from parental authority for more independence, the early adolescent wants to create more room to grow (social freedom) and to assert more individuality (self-expression). On both counts she is more willful to live with and more determined to get her way, even when she makes wrong choices. In willful children, where there's a will, there's a win.

Figuring Out the Stakes

During adolescence, parents, for the sake of safety and responsibility, take more unpopular stands for the young person's best interests against new freedoms he may want. This means there is more frequent disagreement between them. And after some complaining and argument, the adolescent usually consents to live within the limits that parents firmly set.

With a willful early adolescent, however, there are two issues at stake, not one. First is the specific disagreement, about freedom to go bike riding after dark, for example. But second, and equally important, is the principle of winning for its own sake. Losing an argument with parents feels like giving in to their terms and losing face. That's why having the last word feels so important to a strong-willed boy or girl.

When Your Child Constantly Argues to Win

Willful children, particularly in adolescence, are often determined to debate until they win the argument or gain the freedom they want. Arguing to win is the order of the day. So what are parents supposed to do? Should they be equally willful back and refuse to declare defeat?

▶ DID YOU KNOW?

What is the most common willpower that willful children lack? Patience with delayed gratification. Strong-willed children often lack the ability to wait for what they want without complaining or some-how hurrying time along. Willful children believe they "can't wait" for what they want. A parent's job is to teach them that they can.

No. Arguing to win at all costs only encourages the child to do the same. Better to declare "no contest" and take the issue of winning off the table by declaring something like this to your willful adolescent: "After explaining why I want something, I am not going to argue with you about it. After all, whether or not to cooperate with me is always up to you. There's no point in fighting to win your freedom of choice with me because you already have it. Of course, if you choose not to cooperate with me, then I have choices about what I want to do in response." To which declaration the willful child may ask, "Well, what will you do if I go bike riding after dark anyway?" This is when you clarify with your child that the issue is not who wins, but how his or her choices can influence your own. "That's for me to decide, if you choose to go against my will," you explain.

The Issue of When

"When can I have it? Why can't I have it now?" Willful children are often ruled by a desire for immediate gratification. They are inclined to go fast through life, to hurry up rather than to slow down when one of their wants is concerned. Urgently the six-year-old pleads, "I know my birthday is tomorrow, but can't I open one present now? I hate having to wait!" Any delay can seem like torture because every want feels so intense. Where there's a will, there's a when.

DOES THIS SOUND LIKE YOUR CHILD?

Desire for immediate satisfaction ("I can't wait") and attraction to temptation ("I can't resist") often rule the decisions willful children make, sometimes resulting in feelings of regret later. "I wish I had taken the time to think first." "I wish I hadn't let myself be persuaded." These children actually need more willpower—the willpower to be patient and the discipline of self-denial.

How to Endure Impatience

For the willful child, anything worth waiting for is worth having now. When should a want be satisfied? Immediately, if possible. Many willful children lack an important kind of willpower that they will need in life—patience, the capacity to endure delay for what they want or even do without. Willful children who are ruled by impatience are easily frustrated and soon end up angry, using anger when they can to get what they desire.

Parents can teach patience by teaching planning. "Let's think out the steps that need to be taken for you to get that to happen." Parents can teach patience by teaching earning. "When you have completed all your chores, then you get to do what you want."

An Interesting Question—Savers and Spenders

Here's a telling question to consider. When it comes to managing money, is your willful child a spender or a saver? At issue is the management of "when"—when will money be spent, now or later?

Spenders are ruled by pleasure in the moment. If money burns a hole in your child's pocket, then you may have some patience to teach. To help the child delay spending now, see if you can get him to begin saving for something later. Saving requires patience with slow accumulation, regular deposits, and interest growing over time. Saving has material value, but more importantly, it has psychological value. Willpower is used to restrain immediate want in favor of pursuing a long-term objective. Savers demonstrate impulse control and the ability to delay gratification.

The Issue of Whose

Strong-willed children can be proprietary over what they have—be it position, privileges, or possessions. What they want, they want to own. The question "Whose is it?" asks to whom something of value belongs. If it belongs to someone, then that person controls who gets to use it. And willful children usually like to be in control not just of what they do, but also of what they have. Where there's a will, there's a whose.

The Firstborn Child

Consider the oldest child, first born and firmly established in the center of the family, used to having a monopoly on what parents have to give, now having to adjust to another child in the home. At first the oldest was excited by the fantasy of having company, a playmate, someone to take care of. But fantasy soon degenerates into reality when it becomes clear that this younger sibling is a rival for parental attention, approval, time, and family resources. If the youngest is particularly cute and winning, the oldest can become more willful in response. "Whose is the place on the bed between my parents? Mine!" So the oldest starts acting very territorial and possessive and tries to push the young intruder out.

A BETTER PARENTING PRACTICE

A willful child can be very possessive of whose way is "the right way" to get things done. Intolerant of opposing beliefs, the child will insist on "doing it my way!" Parents need to help the willful child accept the legitimacy of other people's lifestyles, value sets, and points of view.

Does Your Firstborn Have Trouble Sharing?

Sharing can be hard to learn for an oldest child who is used to having uncontested access to all parents have to provide. But to get along in the world, everyone must learn to share. To that end, parents teach the child to take turns, to let the other person go first, to compromise, to sacrifice for others, and to sometimes do without. Most important, the willful child needs to be taught that contentment does not depend on having it "all," but on understanding that when it comes to satisfying wants, "some" has to be enough.

In willful children, where there's a will, there's a want, so they can act very intense. Where there's a will, there's a won't, so they can act very stubborn. Where there's a will, there's a why, so they can act very challenging. Where there's a will, there's a win, so they can act very combative. Where there's a will, there's a when, so they can act very impatient. And where there's a will, there's a whose, so they can act very possessive. Willfulness takes a variety of common forms, and parents must be ready to contend with them all.

Chapter 2

Problems Your Child Will Face

Ten Things You Will Learn in This Chapter

- The difference between healthy and unhealthy power.

- How to teach your child tolerance for frustration.

- How to effectively react to your child's serious threats.

- What to say during a tantrum to calm your child down and move forward.

- How a charming child always gets what he/she wants and how to avoid this.

- Why willful children are susceptible to perfectionism.

- About your child's self-esteem issues and his/her "need to win."

- How your child' social dominance at home can tear apart your family.

- Why working in groups can be aggravating for your child.

- How to nurture but not overindulge your child.

Too Powerful?

Willful children are good at getting their way—going after what they want, refusing what they don't want, and getting others to do for them what they don't want to do for themselves.

Supporting healthy power, like ambition, is what parents want to do; supporting unhealthy power, like coercion, they want to avoid. To enable the growth of unhealthy power only makes a hard situation worse and does the child a disservice by encouraging the growth of traits that will cause the child trouble later on.

A BETTER PARENTING PRACTICE

You know your child is powerful to a fault when you back off a healthy stand because you feel overwhelmed by your child's intense insistence or resistance. Remember to hold firm to what you want. And teach your child tolerance for frustration by practicing delay and denial of gratification by saying and meaning "Not now, later" and "No, you can't."

For example, imagine parents who feel like their eight-year-old is running the family. He gets furious when they refuse him what he wants, and he gets so upset that they feel they must finally give in to stop things from getting out of hand. They have to tiptoe around, not asking him to do things when he's in a bad mood. But how has he gotten this way? The parents have allowed it. They have given their power to him and are blaming him for what they've done. When a willful child is powerful to a fault, it is usually with the complicity of parents who have given up sticking to normal demands and setting healthy limits. It takes courage, clarity, and consistency to effectively parent a strong-willed child who will respect nothing less than parental firmness.

Willful Threats

For some parents, there are times when their willful child can be scary. Consider willful threats such as "If you don't let me have what I want . . . :

- "I'll hurt myself!" (at age five)
- "I'll run away!" (at age eight)
- "I'll hate you forever!" (at age ten)

It can feel daunting to face down an intensely upset willful child and hold to the demand or limit that you have imposed, particularly if you have a fearful childhood history of being domineered yourself. But growth is just a gathering of power, from dependence to independence, and it is your responsibility as a parent to help your child gather power in appropriate, and not inappropriate, ways. It is inappropriate to give a willful child's emotional demands extortionate power, as though the child were saying, "If you want me to stop my tantrum, just give me what I want."

Getting Away with What Isn't Wise

Sometimes a willful child can lose by winning. Backing parents off a healthy stand, the child gets to do something that is against the parents' better judgment, and their judgment proves correct. The child lands in trouble from being given freedom unwisely gained. So after her tireless pleading and promising, parents relent and let their daughter go spend the night with a friend who they know has less adult supervision than is wise. And then the two friends sneak out and get picked up by the police at a party that the parents would not have approved of.

DID YOU KNOW?

Giving in to a tantrum rewards emotional extortion. Better to say, "When you are through acting so sad and mad and are willing to talk about how you feel, I am willing to listen. But what I asked you to do [or said you cannot do] still stands."

"It's your fault for letting me go, so you should get me out of this!" protests the child. At this point, parents need to make a clear separation of responsibility. "Yes, letting you go over to your friend's was our responsibility. But what you chose to do there was up to you, and so the consequences are yours to pay." For parents, it may feel easier to give in to their child's willful want now, but if they know it is not wise, they are only borrowing trouble from later on.

Too Controlling?

Like any power, willpower can be hard to limit. The more a child has, the more he becomes accustomed to, the more he wants. There never seems to be enough, because the older the child grows, the larger the world becomes, and the more there is to try and control.

DOES THIS SOUND LIKE YOUR CHILD?

Beware the extremely charming child. The child can use charm for willful effect, being so disarmingly hard to resist, seductively getting what he wants. But the more often charm works, the more willful the child becomes. Very young children who are very cute often learn to use acting cute to get their way. Parents find her darling ways irresistible.

That's what willpower is really about: exercising the ability to control oneself, external events, and others. Control of self can take the form of perfectionism and the drive to perform error-free. Control of events can take the form of managing every situation, imposing and satisfying a personal agenda. Control of others can take the form of insisting on how others are supposed to act and dictating their behavior.

Control of Self

Willful children can be susceptible to perfectionism. They may set personal performance standards that are extremely demanding, tolerate no mistakes, and forgive no failure. Consequently, willful children can be unduly hard on themselves when they don't manage to live up to their very high standards. They can fly into a rage for not performing up to their ideal: "I'm so stupid!" This kind of name-calling can injure self-esteem.

Parents need to intervene at this sign of intense personal pressure to help their child understand the control she should be taking. "When you fail to meet your standard of performance, instead of pressuring yourself to push harder or punishing yourself for not meeting it, we want you to consider a third choice: ask yourself if that standard was realistic. Was it within reach with a reasonable effort? If not, consider lowering it to one that you are more likely to meet. Personal standards are not fixed. They are not genetic. They are chosen. And your responsibility is to set reachable standards that you can meet with reasonable effort. Excessive and unreasonable standards that you set will only cause you stress."

Control of Events

When any disagreement, game competition, or athletic event routinely becomes a "must win" situation, the child's self-esteem may depend on winning. And he can push himself and others very hard and become extremely unhappy when he does not prevail. Losing an argument, getting beaten at a game, or being defeated in sport can cause the child to feel deeply sad or very angry. In tears or in a rage after losing, he literally seems unable to accept defeat. He may be called a poor sport by other children. "He needs to learn to lose," advises the coach.

And as parents, you need to help the highly controlling, highly competitive willful child learn to make a separation between effort and outcome. "It is good to try your best," you can tell him. "So take pride in your effort, but accept that you cannot control how chance and circumstance will unexpectedly influence everybody's play. Understand that the effort you make [which you do control] is no guarantee of the outcome you want [which you don't control]."

DID YOU KNOW?

Parents find themselves getting angry when their willful child is exercising too much control at home, but they are really angry with themselves. They are angry for conceding authority and putting the child—instead of themselves—in charge of what happens in the family.

Control of Others

Parents can feel tyrannized by a willful child when "King Boy" or "Queen Girl" becomes enthroned in the family: "All we can think about is what he's going to want or not want us to do next, and what he'll do if he can't have his way!" Driven by this preoccupation, they direct all their attention to the child, giving up even more control, focusing on what the child is going to want at the expense of considering their own wants. Meanwhile, the child enjoys the dominance he or she has been given.

Social dominance at home is based on two kinds of control. What the child can "make" parents do (command) and what parents *can't* "make" the child do (defiance). Both giving orders and refusing to obey feel empowering. To counter these types of control, parents need to let the child know that he can make requests but he cannot give orders, and that his requests will not automatically or immediately be met. "You can ask what you'd like us to do, but you cannot tell us what to do." As for defiance, parents need to let the child know that when they have made a request, they will keep after its fulfillment until it is met: "You may try to delay doing what we ask, but you cannot get out of doing what we ask, because we will keep after you until you get it done."

➤ DID YOU KNOW?

One reason why willful children can get so upset after losing a competition is that they never considered the possibility of defeat. Wanting to win so badly, they believe that they should win all the time. Parents need to help them modify this unrealistic expectation: "No one wins all the time."

Watch for control-taking behaviors—particularly bullying and bossiness—with her friends or siblings. To the willful child, it can feel like the end (getting what she wants) justifies the means (coercing other people). So your child acts so bossy with her friends that they refuse to come over. Bossiness is offensive and bullying is abusive. In both cases, parents need to call the child's attention to the social damage being done.

That's a common problem for willful children—in going for control with other people, they can focus on their objective at the expense of the relationship. Parents have to keep weighing in on the side of the relationship: "To win your way and lose a friend is not a good bargain."

Too Independent?

Used to getting her own way, the willful child can become accustomed to going her own way, independent of what others say or want. "Don't tell me what to do! Don't tell me how to do it! I'll decide!" The willful child can resent being directed and can resist directions. Willful children are firmly wed to their personal agendas.

Going It Alone

Intent on going her own way, the willful child can be impatient with people getting in her way, which is why many such children shy away from operating in groups and prefer to go it alone, participating in individual sports, not team sports, for example. "I don't like playing on a team because I can't control how others do."

Once she has made up her mind about what she wants, she wants it without any interference. For this reason, many willful children in elementary and middle school find working in groups to be an aggravation. "I hate having to do this project with other people. They just slow me down and what we end up with isn't everything I want. I'd rather just work alone." She really dislikes having her individual achievement depend on the performance of others. But if the group project is unavoidable, the willful child will often take charge of the group, dictating and doing most of the work just to have the project suit her vision and meet her standards. She does what she can to turn "our way" into "my way."

DOES THIS SOUND LIKE YOUR CHILD?

Sometimes the willful child is acting like a puppet on a string, and parents fail to see or fault the puppeteer. Because a willful child can be so easily excited, incited, and upset, another sibling may take advantage of this vulnerability, secretly provoking his or her strong-willed sibling to get this attention-grabbing rival in trouble with parents. Beware a secret aggravator in your family.

As parents, you don't want to deny or depreciate the strength of individuality and independence that your willful child possesses, but you can still talk to her about the importance of learning to cooperate and collaborate as well. Learning to compromise is an essential cooperative and collaborative skill. Remind her of the saying "None of us is as smart as all of us." Tell her, "The more ways you have of looking at a problem, the more broad your understanding becomes. The more different ideas you can include, the richer your project becomes."

This does not discount the individual creativity of your child. It is simply encouraging her to learn the skills of group creativity as well. It is why the willful child who often prefers individual sports should also be given a chance to play and appreciate the possibilities of a team sport. Remind her, "In many situations, people working together can accomplish more than a single person working alone."

Being Difficult to Coach

One common by-product of being independent to a fault is being uncoachable. "I know! I know! I know!" protests the willful child when given explanation or offered instruction. "I can figure it out! Let me do it by myself! I don't need your help!" But after a frustrated or failed experience, the child may belatedly accept your assistance. And that's okay. The child can learn after the fact that accepting help before the fact could have saved some difficulty and distress. Sometimes, the child learns, following parental instructions, and not personal inclinations, is the easier way.

Willing to Try Anything

Often associated with the independent streak that accompanies willfulness is a tendency to be driven by curiosity and challenge. The strong-willed child may be drawn to "try anything," to engage in risk taking to see what many experiences are like, without considering the consequences. Independent of what he has been told, independent of weighing risks involved, eager to challenge himself in a new way, the willful child always seems up for an adventure. "Our son never met a dare he didn't like."

When willfulness carries with it this devil-may-care sense of independence, parents absolutely must allow the child to learn from the adverse consequences of risk taking, should they follow. You must give practical cautions when you know your child is going to take risks. The independent child is determined to learn from experience, which often means learning the hard way—from his or her mistakes.

Too Exceptional?

Parents naturally believe their children are special. In appearance, in precocity, in talent, in charm, in personality, in some characteristic, they believe their child is above the norm or otherwise remarkable. Treating the unique as exceptional, however, can cause the child to believe her own rave reviews, coming to treat herself as her parents see her. "I know I am special because my parents treat me so." She begins to view herself in the mirror of her parents' exaggerated perceptions.

When the child in question is also a strong-willed child, this exceptional treatment can often increase willfulness to harmful effect. Consider two common examples: the overindulged child and the star child.

The Overindulged Child

"All we want to do is make her happy; we adore her so!" And so the smitten parents work to please the child any way they can, satisfying her wants and celebrating her outstanding qualities, until continued indulgence causes her to feel not only very special, but entitled to very special treatment—from attention given to desires gratified to resources provided. When she already happens to be a strong-willed only child, this cultivated sense of entitlement increases existing willfulness. The parents are unwilling to set healthy social, emotional, or financial boundaries, setting the child too free for his or her own good. "I don't have to play by other people's rules! My own are all that matter."

DOES THIS SOUND LIKE YOUR CHILD?

Sometimes a child is so forceful, winning, talented, or precocious that parents encourage her to get away with anything, granting her immunity from rules and responsibilities that other children must abide by. Boasted one such child, whose gifts were allowed to excuse her faults, "I can do no wrong in my parents' eyes." Parents must be on guard against this special treatment.

The problem here is not really so much with the child's overdemanding as it is with the parents' enjoying the pleasure of overindulging their child. Wanting to give to their child is a natural part of loving their child, giving being an expression of that love. They want to do what they can to make their child happy, and they do not want to do anything to make their child unhappy. Parents need to moderate indulgence with a willful child, or that child will start expecting overindulgence as her due. To this end:

- Give the child the gift of not getting everything desired.
- Give the child the gift of having to work for what is wanted.

- Give the child the gift of enjoying giving to others.
- Give the child the gift of knowing that getting some of what one wants, not everything, is good enough.

DOES THIS SOUND LIKE YOUR CHILD

Overindulgence by parents can create a sense of entitlement in the child: "Since I am treated specially, I deserve to be." In turn, entitlement empowers willfulness: "I expect to be given whatever I want."

Preschool and school experiences can be helpful here. Thus, the only child at home has the experience of being treated as one of many at school, learning to delay or do without all the attention that is desired, learning to share with other children, and generally learning to operate on less self-indulgent and entitled terms.

The Star Child

Some willful children perform very well for themselves, developing outstanding athletic, academic, appearance, artistic, leadership, and other capacities that bring a great deal of social approval and attention in response—adults basking in the glory of the high-achieving child. Treated as stars in their small social world, part of the special treatment they receive may be exceptions to normal rules and expectations for celebrity's sake.

Thus, some teachers, basking in the child's reflected glory, may be willing to let a star child's neglected homework assignments be made up late with full credit given instead of the zero that is normally given for missed work. They don't want poor academic performance to jeopardize his outstanding athletic performance on the field of play. Sometimes star students are allowed to break normal social rules, to get special exceptions made, acting outlaw and getting away with it, adults excusing the problem behavior to protect and preserve the prominent child.

A BETTER PARENTING PRACTICE

Willful children who star in some area of performance in their life should be held to the same responsible account as any ordinarily performing child.

Parents also can get caught in the star trap. For example, their straight-A student is doing so well academically that they choose to overlook increasing infractions of rules at home that mask a substance problem they do not suspect. It never occurs to them that a good kid who earns such good grades could get into trouble with drugs. But it happens all the time.

Too Focused on Self?

Preoccupation with what one wants or doesn't want can cause a strong-willed child to spend a lot of attention and energy on himself or herself. This is why strong-willed children are commonly criticized by parents for being extremely self-centered or selfish. "All he ever thinks about is what he wants. It's always 'Me! Me! Me!' What about what other people want? What about us?"

This accusation is often true. Personal wants can feel so urgent and intense that the willful child cannot see beyond them, cannot see that other people have needs and wants as legitimate and important as his. This is why parents have two ongoing issues to address with their willful child: thinking beyond oneself and mutuality.

Thinking Beyond Oneself

Parents of a strong-willed child may sometimes feel that only one person's needs matter, and that person is not either of the parents. The mother who has been playing for over an hour with her strong-willed five-year-old declares an end to the game in order to pick up household tasks put aside for play. "Play with me! I want you to play with me! You never play with me!" objects the child, who sees only her own interrupted wants and has no perception of what else her mother needs to do.

Parents may be disturbed by this insensitivity and unresponsiveness to others that the willful child is demonstrating. "She acts so greedy, as if she's the only one in the relationship that counts, the only one who is even there! As though her needs are the only ones that count. Is she blind? Doesn't she care about the welfare of other people?" The answer to these questions is partly yes and partly no.

Yes, the willful child can be so caught up in the demands of self that the reality of other people's needs is overlooked. No, the child is capable of caring, but she needs to be reminded about what else to care about. For this reason, when a willful child acts self-focused to a fault, parents have to help the child see beyond herself, to understand and appreciate the needs and wants of other people, too. "I know you're disappointed that I am ending our play. Why am I stopping the game now? Think about it. Pretend you are me and tell me what else I might be wanting or needing to do for myself."

DID YOU KNOW?

One way to moderate a willful child's excessive self-centeredness is to regularly involve that boy or girl in community service. Learning from the plight of people less fortunate can lessen the willful child's self-preoccupation, while volunteering can become an object lesson in placing the needs of others before the needs of oneself.

Mutuality

When willful children enter adolescence around ages nine to thirteen, they tend to become more willful still because early adolescence, with its social separation from family and push for more independence, is a very self-centering period of growth. At this time, if parents let growth tendencies prevail, their relationship with their child may be increasingly on one-way terms; that is, the child's way. "It's all for him and nothing for us! It's all giving on our side and nothing but taking on his!" If parents allow this condition to continue, they will end up resenting their child. Instead, they should insist on living in a two-way relationship. They should insist on mutuality.

Mutuality in a relationship means that the needs of both parties are recognized and respected in three ways.

1. There is reciprocity, which means that each person acts in the relationship to contribute to the other's good.
2. There is compromise, which means that when a difference in wants arises, each party is willing to go beyond his or her immediate self-interest to create a solution that both can support.
3. There is consideration, which means that both parties, knowing each other's sensitivities so well, do not purposefully attack each other's vulnerabilities.

In a family where a willful adolescent has come to rule:

- When it comes to reciprocity, she appears to believe, "My needs are the only ones that count."
- When it comes to compromise, she appears to believe, "My way is the only way I will accept."
- When it comes to sensitivity, she appears to believe, "My feelings matter and yours are of no concern."

When parents find themselves in a one-way (his way) relationship with their ruling child, they have helped to create a "spoiled" child. In his ignorance, the child may feel that getting parents to live entirely on his terms is good, but it is not. It will spoil him for later caring relationships with people who, unlike parents who are committed to stick around out of love and obligation, will refuse to live in a relationship where a healthy exchange of mutuality is not observed.

A primary responsibility of parents with a willful child is to foster the child's ability to participate in loving relationships by insisting that he or she live with them on two-way, mutual terms. With their ruling willful child, parents must take a stand for mutuality for their own sake and for the long-term interest of the child. If parents don't want to live with a terminally self-serving child or adolescent who is all take and no give, then they must take strong stands to bring mutuality back into the relationship.

To reestablish reciprocity…
Let the child know that for parents to give, they must first receive. "We're happy to do for you, but only after you've done for us."

To reestablish compromise…
Let the child know that agreements have to work in the interests of both parties to the agreement. "For us to give some to you on this, you are going to have to give some to us."

To reestablish sensitivity in the relationship…
Let the child know that any inconsiderate or hurtful words or acts will stop the flow of resources, services,

and permissions until amends are made. "We don't treat you that way, and we expect that you will not treat us that way, either."

DID YOU KNOW?

Parents who consent to live in a one-way relationship with their child (giving in to her way all the time and rarely getting their way) end up resenting the willful child for being dictatorial. Their resentment is misplaced. It is really up to the parents to insist that the child live on two-way terms.

Too Intolerant?

Used to wanting his own way, used to pushing for his own way, used to believing that his way is the right way, a willful child can be intolerant of other people's ways and of changes that occur when either conflicts with his own way. "That's not how you're supposed to do it!" "This is not what's supposed to happen!" "My way is the right way!"

Inclined to be dictatorial when it comes to knowing the proper approach or desired outcome, the willful child can be intolerant to a fault, that intolerance expressed in inflexibility.

Inflexibility

When it comes to change, most willful children like to dictate how the process unfolds and what outcome is reached. "When we start getting ready to move, I want to be the one to put my things in boxes, and when we get in the new apartment, I want to choose how to decorate my room." And parents may agree with these requests because they serve the larger purpose of moving and getting settled in.

Lots of life changes, however, are less susceptible to the child's power of control, which is why change causes her to feel out of control, anxious, and angry on that account. "The new school is completely different from the one I was used to. I hate it! I won't go back!" But going on strike against unwanted change does not make change go away. Rigidity, refusing to change to adjust to change, is not the answer. Flexibility and adaptability are what the willful child needs to learn. To that end, parents must encourage and coach the child to make the best of a hard situation, mourning what has been lost leaving the old school, then looking for the unexpected benefits that are waiting to be found in the new one. "There are gifts in every adversity," you can explain, "and we will help you take advantage of new possibilities and discover new friends."

Every gift is double-edged. For every strength that parents nurture in their child, some degree of liability is created. Hence, the child who feels secure in knowing exactly what his parents expect of him, enjoying consistent family routines, being able to rely on his parents' commitments, and having a sense of personal control, can come to count on this vital support in a rigid way and have trouble adapting to change.

- "But you never told me this might happen; this isn't fair!" (And there are violated expectations.)
- "But we've always done it this way; I don't want to change!" (And there are violated household routines.)
- "But you promised; you can't go back on your word!" (And there are violated parental commitments.)
- "But I don't like not being in charge; it isn't fun!" (And there are violated personal controls.)

Teaching Flexibility

In their desire to create security at home, parents may inadvertently reduce their child's capacity to deal with the normal chaos of life caused by unanticipated events, revised plans, broken agreements, and circumstances over which no one has control. Hence the parents' dilemma: how to give the child security and teach flexibility at the same time? The answer is partly in the question, "Flexibility must be taught—but how?"

Within the sheltered social reality of family, parents can teach flexibility by approaching some events expectation-free.

- Child: "What will it be like when we get there? What will we do?"
- Parent: "I don't know exactly. We'll just have to see what it's like and then figure out what we want to do."

Parents can treat routines themselves as partly flexible.

- Child: "Why aren't you going to read me a bed-time story tonight?"
- Parent: "Because I'm tired and really need to get to bed myself. Maybe there's a way for you to do a bedtime story for yourself instead."

Parents can treat their commitments as what they want and mean to do, but cannot always guarantee.

- Child: "But you said we could, you did!"
- Parent: "I meant the promise when I made it, but that was before everyone got sick. I still want to keep that promise, but now we'll have to do it another time."

Protection is no preparation. Sheltering that focuses only on security at home may set the child up for some hard adjustments in the outside world, where flexibility to adjust is necessary for healthy survival. Change is the law of all living things.

Chapter 3

Problems You Will Face as a Parent

Ten Things You Will Learn in This Chapter

- How your personality affects your strong-willed child's.

- How to determine if you are a strong-willed person, yourself!

- What, within your own personality, is in your power to change.

- About how strong the power of imitation can be.

- What your child's picky eating has to do with being strong-willed.

- How to avoid a simple situation, like making the bed, from escalating into an all-out battle.

- About timing and creating a delay can enhance understanding.

- How constantly defending your authority can hurt your relationship with your child.

- About yelling and what purpose it has in parenting.

- How worry can become toxic and overparenting can get in the way!

41

Characteristics That Define a Strong-Willed Parent

Through inheritance, imitation, and interaction, strong-willed parents often beget strong-willed children. If you were born strong-willed, there is some likelihood that one or more of your children will innately acquire that self-determined characteristic. If you model strong-willed behavior, there is some likelihood that one or more of your children may identify with your willful ways and react in kind. The person you present is a more powerful influence on them than the parenting you provide. Your way of being with yourself, with other people, and with the world all communicate the example that you set and that the child follows, both of you mostly unaware of what is being given and what is being learned.

Know thyself. This is probably the most important requirement for being an effective communicator and disciplinarian, because then you understand the human nature you have to work with (what you can actually control) when parenting your child. There is nothing inherently wrong with being a strong-willed parent, any more than there is anything inherently wrong with being a strong-willed child. In fact, as you have seen, there is much "right" to be valued that accompanies such self-determination.

What is "wrong," however, is for parents not to recognize their own strong-willed characteristics, because then ignorance may lead them to cause and compound problems with their own willful child. "I don't understand why my son argues with me all the time and feels he has to have the last word! I've argued with him about it for as long as I can remember, but for some reason, he just won't change. But neither will I!" In this situation, the parent really doesn't understand his complicity in encouraging the problem he is complaining about. Like father, like son, but because the father is unaware of his willful nature and behavior, he can't see how he has acted to help create the problem with his son and to make it worse.

A BETTER PARENTING PRACTICE

A strong-willed parent who believes he or she can "defeat" a strong-willed child is sadly mistaken. A parent who rules by making threats and issuing ultimatums will continually collide with a head-strong child who proudly refuses to be bossed around. To avoid this costly conflict, the adult must be flexible, not rigid, request cooperation and not just command compliance, and aim to resolve inevitable human differences in nonvolatile ways.

Are You Strong-Willed?

Here's a chance to make a rough self-assessment to see if perhaps you are a strong-willed parent. How many of these statements apply to you?

- I don't take no for an answer.
- I don't back down to anyone.
- I hate losing an argument.

- I don't like changing my routine for other people.
- Once I make up my mind, I stick with it.
- Once I start something, I finish it.
- When I make a commitment, I keep it.
- When in disagreement, I tend to listen with my mind made up.
- I like to take the time to do things right.
- I get upset when I make mistakes.
- I don't like admitting mistakes.
- I don't like to apologize.
- I like other people to do things my way.
- I try to be perfect.
- I expect other people to live up to my standards.
- I don't give up.
- I will win at all costs.
- I need to know everything that is going on.
- I don't trust other people to take care of my business.
- I never admit defeat.
- I like to play by my rules, and I like others to as well.
- I'd rather give help than receive it.
- I don't like being told I'm wrong.

Obviously, this is not an exhaustive list of strong-willed characteristics. However, if you checked off a majority of them, you might consider that you could be a strong-willed parent.

Becoming Less Strong-Willed

Look back at any of the characteristics you checked off. Most of them are within your power to change. And you might choose to change in those instances where your willful behavior is triggering a similar willful response in your child. For example, you find yourself in an ongoing similarity conflict with your daughter. You won't admit defeat or back down, and neither will she. You are both extremely stubborn. Aware of this, you have a choice. Either you can keep doing this dance of stubbornness with your daughter every time a disagreement arises, or you can change your own behavior and introduce a different step. "We certainly do view what your friend did in different ways. I'd like to hear more about your take on her behavior; then I'd like to tell more about mine." So you introduce the new step of discussing to understand in place of the old step of arguing to win.

DID YOU KNOW?

Strong-willed parents and a willful child must work out a compromise between what parents want to have happen and what the child is willing to do. Parents who are rigidly uncompromising often raise a child who learns to be the same.

You Teach What You Are

On the plus side, a strong-willed parent communicates a well-defined presence to respond to, so a child knows where that parent stands and what behavior to expect from that parent. On the negative side, a strong-willed parent often encourages, by imitation and interaction, a strong-willed response from a child who, if not born willful, can learn to become that way.

The Power of Imitation

Many parents believe they provide a single model of behavior that their child is influenced, by example, to follow. This belief is not true. Actually, each parent provides *two* models to follow, not one—how to be and how not to be. So your child may pick up your sense of humor and the enjoyment of getting people to laugh, but may elect not to incorporate your use of sarcasm, which can sometimes humiliate and hurt. "I like my mom's way of clowning around and being silly, but I don't like when she uses it to put people down."

▶ DID YOU KNOW?

A good example of the power of imitation is the following quote: "I learned to be so stubborn by refusing to give in to my father, who was the most stubborn person I have ever known." As you can see, conflict can create resemblance.

Strong-willed parents can be unaware how imitation of their ways is at the root of their problems with the willful child. For example, consider parents who believe their rules should be obeyed who have a daughter who, according to them, has no respect for rules at all. They complain, "She doesn't believe in following rules—ours or anybody else's!"

But they have underestimated the power of imitation. Just because their daughter opposes the parents' rules doesn't mean she doesn't believe in rules. In fact, the opposite is the case—she has learned from her parents that following rules is extremely important. So important that she has made up her own rules and, like her parents, will stick to them no matter what. The real problem is, her rules are different from their rules. The challenge is to discuss and create a set of rules they can all subscribe to, at the same time consenting to go along with some of her rules if she will consent to go along with some of theirs.

As parents change their model, the child often changes in response. Parents who are alcoholic or otherwise addicted, for example, often become strong-willed—self-centered and controlling to a fault. Identifying with these personal characteristics, although not using the substance, a child can become willful in similar ways—thoughtless and demanding of others. When, however, the alcoholic parent enters recovery and begins to live differently within himself and with others, becoming more sensitive and considerate to live with, the child has a different model of behavior to imitate, and often does.

The Power of Interaction

It is a peculiar irony about nurturing a strong-willed child that the same willful outcome can be achieved from opposing kinds of parenting. A strong-willed child can emerge as easily from oppressive parenting as from parenting of the permissive kind. With an oppressive parent bent on dictatorial control, a child can strengthen willpower by regularly opposing overbearing parental authority. Excessive parental restriction can make more freedom well worth fighting for.

With a permissive parent (and also with a neglectful or overindulgent parent), a child can be given so much power of choice over what he gets to do, and what he gets to have, that self-determination becomes the only authority he or she will obey. Excessive personal choice can create intolerance for parental limits and restraints.

When parents complain that their willful child is a fussy eater, they usually have only themselves to blame, for example. By being given flexible food choices when what has been prepared is not the child's favorite, the child learns to eat only what she likes and to refuse what she does not.

DID YOU KNOW?

A good example of the power of interaction is the following quote: "Because my parents were never satisfied with how I did, I ended up becoming very critical of myself." How we are treated is how we learn to treat ourselves.

In general, it is best that parents don't turn mealtime into a battle of wills: "You will sit at this table for however long it takes you to eat what has been put in front of you!" Better to eliminate any alternative eating choice. When parents consistently withdraw the option of something else to eat, food fussiness usually disappears. "This is what has been prepared. You can choose to eat it or not. However, if you choose not to, then you may find yourself having to go hungry until the next meal because we are not fixing you anything else, and there will be no snacks allowed."

The Question of Now or Later

For strong-willed parents, time can be a problem. Part of their agenda, in addition to determining the rules, priorities, and schedule that the child is expected to observe, is demanding the child do what the parents want when asked, which means "Now!" In service of this need for immediacy, strong-willed parents can face difficulty in two ways: with intolerance for delay and with incapacity to create delay.

Intolerance for Delay

Strong-willed parents don't like having their requests and demands put off by a child who is more interested in continuing to do something else. "I will in a minute!" objects the child. "You'll do it when I ask," replies the parent, growing impatient, "and that means now!"

Impatience is a form of frustration that can soon lead to irritation. It causes parents to be vulnerable to emotional reactions, when rational responses would serve them better. An impatient parent with an impatient child usually leads to an angry outcome, and the issue between parent and child becomes more emotionally inflamed. Now a simple matter of making a bed becomes an angry interchange about unreasonable demands (the child's complaint) and who's in charge (the parent's issue).

When a child, particularly an adolescent, discovers that delaying compliance is a predictable button she can push to get an impatient, irritable, or angry parental response, the young person will use power of delay to manipulate you to her benefit. "It's easy to get my dad upset. All I have to do is put off what he wants, when he wants it done." Don't be trapped by your impatience. Just coolly keep after what you want until you get it.

A BETTER PARENTING PRACTICE

Always keep in mind the kind of parent you would like to be, the kind that would cause you to feel good about yourself. Don't rush your parenting. Take whatever time you need to fit that self-affirming role. Treat your child well to treat yourself well.

Incapacity to Create Delay

One operating principle for some strong-willed parents is to tackle a problem with their child as soon as it arises. So, when an infraction occurs, parents believe they must make an immediate decision about a consequence: "You didn't stay off the phone and do your homework as I asked and you agreed, therefore you are grounded from the phone for the next week!" But by responding so quickly, the parent didn't take time to fully investigate the offense as the child explains and complains: "I was just using the phone to get some of the assignment I forgot to write down. You're not being fair!"

Some strong-willed parents have a tendency to "shoot from the lip." They react too quickly. They decide impulsively instead of giving themselves time to think, and then they end up with a decision that is ill-advised. They don't delay long enough to consider what really happened and what is best to do, because they feel delay is a sign of uncertainty, when in fact it shows judgment. "So what are you going to do, not let me go out?" asks the child, impatient to be told. "Why won't you tell me now?" "Because," answers the parent, "I don't have to decide now. I'll take my own good time. You will just have to wait to find out my decision. That's part of your consequence for doing what you shouldn't."

DID YOU KNOW?

When you impulsively make an inappropriately severe disciplinary response, give yourself freedom to retract and modify the decision. It's a lesson not lost on the child: parents can make, admit, and correct mistakes, too. "I was tired from work and overreacted to what you did and I would like to change what I said. Just cleaning up the mess you made is consequence enough."

If you believe that any parenting problem must be resolved right now, or any response to your child's demand must be made right now, then you are in danger of becoming trapped in the moment without sufficient time and space for reflective choice. Whenever you feel jammed into make a parenting decision right now, resolve to grant yourself a delay for time to think. The purpose of delay is deliberation.

Everyday Power Struggles

Strong-willed parents want to be in charge, and they can resort to extreme measures to establish that they are. "I will do whatever it takes to prove that I am the boss in this family and not my child!" Typically, strong-willed parents enjoy unquestioned authority during their son's or daughter's life up to about age nine or ten. This is the age of command, when the parents believe they should be able to do the telling, and the child believes he or she must do what he or she is told. The compliant child does not question parental authority. Both parents and child agree that the parent is in charge.

Come the onset of adolescence, however, between ages nine and thirteen, some degree of change typically occurs. The child leaves the age of command and enters the age of consent, going from believing "you can tell me" to believing "you can't make me or stop me." Now willing to challenge parental authority, the child now understands that parents are powerless to make him do anything without his cooperation or consent.

For strong-willed parents, this change demands an unwelcome adjustment. They do not like their loss of control, and they often resent the early adolescent for diminishing their power. In response, they can overreact in a couple of self-defeating ways: engaging in isometric encounters and losing control to get control. For authoritarian parents who have been used to automatic obedience and were brought up strictly themselves, a compliant child entering a more resistant adolescence can create quite a challenge: "It's gotten to the point where I have to do battle with my daughter just to get her to pick up her room!"

A BETTER PARENTING PRACTICE

Strong-willed parents who insist on always being "right" can end up doing wrong by ignoring relevant information and discounting constructive suggestions from the child because they are so busy defending their authority. Instead of treating the child as an opponent when it comes to resolving a difference, treat the child as a collaborator with whom to solve a common problem.

Isometric Encounters

"I'll show you who's boss! You don't leave the supper table until I say!" and the angry parent physically forces the child to stay seated while the child struggles to stand up, at last giving up resistance because the parent is larger and stronger. So the strong-willed parent has won, right? Wrong.

The parent has prevailed at the moment; but to his detriment in the long term. He allowed an isometric encounter to occur. Isometrics is a strength-building exercise. Pushing as hard as you can against a fixed resistance, you strengthen your power of push. In the supper table confrontation between stubborn father and stubborn daughter described previously, she has pushed as hard as she can against a stronger resistance, losing for the moment, but now stronger than she was before and more resolved to win the next encounter. The strong-willed parent has only increased his daughter's strength of opposition.

DID YOU KNOW?

Never get trapped in an isometric encounter with your strong-willed child. You don't need a more powerful opponent than you already have. Instead, declare your stand, recognize your child's disagreement, put a delay on discussion until you have cooled down, and then return to work out the difference at issue between you.

Losing Control to Get Control

"I just lost control," apologized the parent for having said some ugly things in anger to her son, when he wouldn't immediately interrupt his video game to give help she had requested. But angry words and the damage they inflict cannot be undone by an apology. At most, they will not be repeated as part of the amends the apology makes. Now both parent and child feel hurt because of what she had said in order to get what she wanted.

Strong-willed parents who are determined to "win at all costs" are most at risk of losing control to get control. The parent or child or both end up sorry for how the parent overreacted. A parent, no matter how strong-willed, is not always going to get her way, right away, exactly the way she wants it. That is not a problem to fix; it is a reality to accept.

Yelling is a good example of a bad parenting practice. Yelling is losing control to get control. The battered child ends up in control because he is given the power to provoke the parent into acting so loudly upset. Parents who regularly yell to get their way give away far more power of control then they ever get.

Grasping for Control

Although actual parental control of the child is an illusion (because the child is governed by personal choices that only the child is empowered to make), some strong-willed parents insist on believing that control of their child could or should be so. To prove this illusion true, they will often to go to excessive lengths to prevent what they don't want or to get what they do want. A common example is the fear-prone parent who wants to protect the child from possible harm by reducing exposure to potential risk. Driven by fear, this parent is in danger of becoming overprotective and inclined to excessive control.

The Fear-Prone Parent

Growth requires trying oneself out in ways one has not tried before, and trial-and-error learning always offers potential harm. The toddler can't learn to walk without risking falling down, the eight-year-old can't learn to cook without risking getting burned, the thirteen-year-old can't have a peer group without risking getting in trouble, and the sixteen-year-old can't drive a car without risking having accidents. Growth is an inherently risky process.

DID YOU KNOW?

Parents preoccupied with fear of potential harm to their child can become extremely cautious and overprotective. In consequence, they may raise a child who is anxiously risk-averse or raise a willful child who is rebelliously risk-attracted (too defiantly adventurous for her own good). Instead, parents should simply teach the child how to assess and safely manage risks that come with normal growth.

Parents who cannot bear the thought of exposing their growing child to possible harm can let fear cause them to hold on to the child too tightly, micromanaging the child's behavior, holding growth back instead of letting go so healthy expression, activity, association, and exploration can occur. Of course, letting go is the hardest part of parenting because putting the child at the mercy of his or her immature decision making, much less at the mercy of an unpredictable and dangerous world, is scary for most parents to do. What excites the child ("I can't wait to swim over at the neighbor's pool!") can terrify the fearful parent ("Suppose there's insufficient adult supervision?").

Constructive Worry

To help ease the fear of letting go, the overprotective parent needs to use fear not as a warden who says no to every new freedom because it entails risk, but as an advisor who helps make it safer to let go. Overprotective parents need to avail themselves of constructive worry. Constructive worry asks "what if?" questions to anticipate possible risks and come up with strategies for preventing some and for coping with others should they occur. Asks the parent, "What if the supervising adult was called away from the pool for an emergency, what would you do?" Answers the child, after thinking ahead, "I'd get out of the pool and wait until the parent or another adult came back." Constructive worry can help the child be prepared.

Rather than protect against risks associated with their child's normal growth by forbidding any uncertain exposure, parents can use worry to assess risks, to help the child foresee them, and to teach the child to use worry to think ahead and make plans for dealing with problems that might occur.

Fear-prone parents are high-control parents who have excessive information needs: "I need to know everything that is going on in my child's life to protect him from harm and to feel secure myself." If they get into toxic worry, the more extreme and urgent their need to know becomes, the more their worry discourages the communication they are desperate to have from their child, the more anxious from ignorance they become. For her own protection, the child reduces contact and limits conversation to keep this poisonous anxiety away. "I hate having to listen to my parents' fears. Instead of helping me feel confident, they just encourage me to feel afraid!"

Strong-willed parents can be their own worst enemies or their own best friends. To be the latter, take your strength of will and invest it in patience, persistence, and perspective, three parenting characteristics that shall serve you very well.

Chapter 4

Adapting and Cooperating— Methods for Parenting

Ten Things You Will Learn in This Chapter

- How to handle criticism and comments about your misbehaving child.

- About the difference between parental power and parental influence.

- About the important elements that you must control in your child's life.

- How your attitude can affect your child's ineffective choices.

- To ask yourself, "how can I alter my own behavior to encourage my child to change?"

- Which elements you cannot control—so you can stop trying!

- How the definition of "cooperation" may change when it comes to your child.

- About the two forms of willingness and why you should reward both!

- How to establish a basic system of instructions through experience.

- How to ensure cooperation with a contract!

Parental Control—Is It an Illusion?

The more willful the child, the more preoccupied with control parents tend to become. "How can we get him to start doing what we want?" "How can we get her to stop doing what we don't want?" "How can we make clear that we are in charge?" Getting your strong-willed child to cooperate with what you want can feel like it's taking a monumental effort on your part. You must learn how to teach your child the willingness to work with you, not against you.

DID YOU KNOW?

Parental discipline is not a matter of always getting your way; it is a matter of continually trying to find ways to persuade the child to live within your rules and according to your family values. In this process, you will win some, lose some, compromise a lot, and let a lot of small stuff go.

Since raising a child is such a challenge to undertake, parents want power commensurate with this serious responsibility. Responsibility without control can cause parents to feel helpless, frustrated, afraid, embarrassed, and even ashamed. "Can't you make your daughter behave?" asks an indignant stranger in the store, irritated by the four-year-old who won't stop excitedly running around. And most parents take this as a criticism personally meant. "They're right," parents think. "What's the matter with us? We can't control our child!"

Not being able to control your child is not a problem. It is a reality that parents accept early on if they are wise and honest enough to admit it. For example, arriving home from the hospital with her parents, the little child starts wailing. Alarmed, new parents wonder what is wrong and what is right to do. Believing they must do something to stop the crying, one of them gently picks up the little child and rocks her, all the while mumbling sweet assurances. When, after a couple of minutes, the baby ceases to cry, the triumphant parent congratulates himself: "I stopped her crying!"

A BETTER PARENTING PRACTICE

If parents can't control their child, what can they do? They can control themselves. Parenting is the ongoing process of making choices to influence decisions children make. To change their child's behavior, parents must be willing to examine and change their own.

On second thought, however, he admits that, for whatever internal cause, the baby chose to stop crying. Now he acknowledges the fundamental law of parenting: the child's behavior is always going to be up to the child. At most, as a parent, he can choose to try and influence choices the child makes.

There is a world of difference between the parent who believes in control and the parent who believes in influence. The first parent gets frustrated when attempts to control the child's behavior fail; the second parent keeps patiently trying different responses in the hopes of finding something instructive or corrective that may work. Parents who cannot accept their powerlessness and let go the illusion of control spend a lot of time feeling angry at, in conflict with, or overreacting to their strong-willed son or daughter.

A BETTER PARENTING PRACTICE

If, despite correction, your child continues to misbehave, then you know you are doing something wrong. Your negative attitude may be arousing a resistant response, your ineffective choices may lack influential power, or you may be enabling conduct you wish to stop. Don't focus on your child's actions, focus on your own: "How can I alter my own behavior to encourage my child to change?"

What Parents Do Control

Certainly parents control some important elements in their child's life. Demonstrating control of these elements can definitely have influential effect.

- Positive and negative treatment given: "Without my parents' encouragement, I wouldn't have tried again."
- Services and resources provided: "Unless I pick up my dirty clothes, my parents say I'll have to wash them myself."
- Freedoms and privileges allowed: "If I do all of my chores this week without having to be

reminded, I'll get to take a friend out for a treat this weekend."

- Expectations and rules to live by: "The only reason I keep doing homework, even though I hate it, is because I'm supposed to do my best."

Of course, what parents are really controlling in each of these situations are their own choices, hoping to influence the choices their child makes.

Loss of Self-Consciousness

When parents feel they have "lost control" of their child, what has really happened is that they have lost something in themselves. They have suffered a loss of self-consciousness. For example, they have become totally preoccupied with their willful fifteen-year-old's free-spending ways. The problem as they see it is that she is totally "irresponsible," constitutionally unable to make her allowance last the week for which it was intended.

No matter how often they explain and explain, by Thursday or Friday, she is back asking for money again. "What's the matter with her?" they ask. What they don't ask is "What's the matter with us?" The problem isn't that their impulsive daughter keeps running out of money. The problem is their own impulsive behavior. When she runs out, they immediately give her more. They're blaming her for irresponsibility that they're encouraging by irresponsibility of their own—refusing to let her suffer the consequences of her decisions.

The first commandment of effective parenting is "Parent, know thyself." The parents who yell at the child to stop yelling are only teaching the child to yell. Always ask yourself, "Am I modeling the behavior I want my child to stop?" The parents who resolve to punish the child until his attitude improves only increase the negativity they wish to reduce. Always ask yourself, "Am I behaving in a self-defeating way?" The parents who rescue the child from consequences of bad choices made are only supporting the continuation of bad choices. Always ask yourself, "Am I enabling behavior I wish to stop?"

What Parents Don't Control

It helps for parents to recognize areas of influence they don't control that contribute to how their child develops or "turns out." Parenting is only one of many significant factors that impact the course of a child's life. Placing excessive faith in parenting causes parents to presume too much control. Treat parenting as important but not all-important. It is not all-powerful; it is simply one source of influence among many. Consider just a few factors parents don't control:

- The impulses the child has or choices the child makes
- The child's inherited human nature—physical vulnerabilities and strengths, innate capacities, temperament, and personality
- The child's rate or course of developmental growth
- The child's social experiences away from home
- The popular culture that shapes the child's values and tastes

- The local and larger history that unfolds over the course of the child's growing up
- Pressures from peers
- Chance events that can alter the child's life for good or ill

Cooperation Is Key

When parenting a strong-willed child, the objective is neither to break the child's will nor conquer the child's won't, because in either case, parents risk crushing or hardening the child's self-determined spirit. Instead, the task for parents is to continually work for the child's willingness to go along with what parents want and don't want. Willingness is cooperation.

In this process, parents need to respect the child's power of choice, appreciate when willingness is given, not overreact when it is not given, keep perspective when problems arise, and be patient and persistent in pursuit of the demands and limits they need met.

Rewarding Willingness

Willingness comes in two forms: going along with what parents want and refraining from doing what parents don't want. Your job is to reward acts of willingness with positive recognition whenever they occur. Relational rewards (like appreciation, approval, affection, and praise) are more powerful than concrete rewards (like freedoms, privileges, objects, or money). While your relationship carries on, concrete rewards will soon be spent or will lose the child's interest. Thus, your child may really want that new accessory for his computer, but he does not want it nearly as much as he wants your approval—to shine in your eyes.

DID YOU KNOW?

Frustrated parents who label a child "selfish," "spoiled," and "inconsiderate" for possessing a strong will risk having the child turn parental disapproval into personal shame: "I'm a bad person, my parents always told me so."

Unfortunately, many parents seem most aware of willingness when they don't get it, taking it for granted when they do. By not rewarding acts of willingness that are given, parents end up losing a chance to encourage their continuation.

Even though your nine-year-old has delayed, disputed, and dragged out your three-minute housekeeping request for over an hour before finally getting it taken care of, that doesn't justify your treating completion with impatience: "Well, it's about time!" Always express appreciation when willingness is given: "Thank you for getting it done."

Keeping the Larger View in Mind

Sometimes desperate parents of a willful child, who seems to oppose them at every turn and to run totally free of their restraint, come to mistakenly believe that he never gives them any willingness at all: "He's a wild child; he never does what we want!" This statement is emotionally true (because that is how parents feel), but it is factually false (because almost no child is 100 percent unwilling).

At this juncture, parents need to take a time-out to let emotion subside enough for a realistic perspective to take hold. Think about it. If a child acted unwilling all the time, then parents would be without any influence. No behavior they wanted would occur, and no behavior they did not want to occur would go undone. How frightening! Parents can really scare themselves by conjuring up such a vision of total ineffectiveness.

A BETTER PARENTING PRACTICE

When you take for granted or ignore a child's act of willingness, you reduce the likelihood that it will be repeated. The child does not feel that his effort is valued. "Why should I keep doing what you ask if you never appreciate what I do?" thinks the child.

So the parents of this "wild child" are exhausted and anxious and believe their parenting is bankrupt. They feel like failures, and their presentation of themselves communicates very low self-esteem. "We're fighting a losing battle morning, noon, and night. Trying to get him up and ready for school each day takes everything both of us have to give. We have to argue and chase him around the house just to get him dressed, fed, homework packed for school, and in the car." But do they thank him for getting dressed, eating breakfast, getting ready for school, and for getting in the car? No, because they feel those are things that he is supposed to do, and in fact, they may even get angry that he doesn't do them "on time." But these parents are not taking advantage of all those opportunities to reinforce the willingness they get and so encourage more of the willingness they want. And getting angry simply gives him power to arouse their emotions, power that he should not have but is probably glad to take.

DOES THIS SOUND LIKE YOUR CHILD?

No willful child is completely unwilling to go along with everything parents want and do not want done. If parents will take the time to calm down and rationally inventory all the kinds of willingness—given on time or after a while—that they are still being shown, they will usually find their child's unwillingness is the exception, not the rule.

In most cases, parents do not see and fully appreciate all the willingness they are being given. Take the parents in the above example. Their child behaves appropriately as a passenger in the car—not yelling, hitting, refusing to sit still, or throwing things. But why does he not behave badly? "Because we've taught him those kinds of behaviors make our driving unsafe," the parents say. So they grudgingly admit that they are being given more willingness than they are giving the child credit for. But how did they teach him to behave safely in the car? "By being extremely firm and clear and consistent about what we wanted and why," they respond.

And with this description, the parents have located, within all their frustrated efforts, a successful example of, and formula for, effective parenting with this strong-willed child. The next time they feel like their wild child is unmanageable, they must ask themselves, "With the current problem, are we being as firm, clear, and consistent as we need to be?"

How to Motivate Cooperation

As soon as parents discern that their child is extremely self-determined to direct, persist, resist, and to prevail, they need to begin training the headstrong boy or girl in the basics of family cooperation. Cooperation is the willingness they want, and it can and must be taught.

Encouraging the Practice of Cooperation

On a daily basis, parents are well advised to consistently initiate seven kinds of cooperative demands. On each occasion, they then need to follow through with insistence until those demands are met, and they need to reward the willful child with some combination of appreciation, approval, and praise for cooperation given.

Consider these basic training demands, which require the child's cooperation in order to be fulfilled:

- Share what you have: "Take turns with that so each of you has a chance to play with it."
- Tell me the truth: "Give me adequate and accurate information about what is going on."
- Listen to me: "When I am talking to you, give me your attention."

- Keep your agreements: "Do what you promised me."
- Be of assistance: "Give me your help."
- Follow directions: "Do it the way I have described."
- Obey the rules: "Remember how you're supposed to act."

Contracting

Because willful children are often so preoccupied with what they want, they can decide to act without being mindful of what you want from them. After a while, parents can feel they are coming out on the losing end of this competition of wants more often than not. Sometimes contracting can encourage cooperation.

So at the beginning of the day you take the time with your child to list out a lot of the things that she is going to want you to do for her—services and resources you will provide. Then you list out a lot of the things you will be wanting from her—acts of help and cooperation she can provide. Then turn this into a contract. "I will be happy to do these things for you, and I will expect you to do these things for me? Agreed?" In most cases, the child will agree to get the matter over with and to get on with her day. But to show you are serious, and if you have cause to believe she will "forget" the morning conversation tonight, write it down and both sign it. This way, when evening resistance arises—"I never said I'd help you fold the laundry!"—you have a written document to back up your request.

DID YOU KNOW?

If by the age of two your child reveals himself to be willful, you must consistently (on a daily basis) initiate demands to cooperate in order to convince the child through practice that cooperation with parents is a normal part of family life. Practice is the foundation of habits, and you want your willful child to learn the habit of cooperating with you.

Making Cooperative Choices

The simplest way to train a child to cooperate is to establish basic systems of instruction through experience. Children must learn that there is a connection between choice and consequence. They must learn through experience that for every choice the child makes about cooperating (or not cooperating) with you, a consequence from you will follow. In general, the choice of willingness to go along with what you want will yield a positive response (consequence) from you. A choice of unwillingness will not yield a positive consequence from you, and may even provoke a negative one.

There are common *choice/consequence connections* parents frequently use to encourage willingness in their child; some are positive and some are negative.

Positive Systems

In general, when it comes to encouraging willingness, positive consequences work better than negative ones because of their long-term impact on the child's desire to work with you. Over time, receiving mostly positive responses increases the value of the relationship for the child, whereas receiving mostly negative responses tends to reduce it: "Why should I do what you want when all you ever do is punish me?"

Positive systems for using the choice/consequence connection to encourage willingness include:

- Using recognition systems, parents positively respond with appreciation, approval, affection, or praise to every act of willingness that they are aware of receiving from the child. "Thanks for remembering to bring in the trash."
- Using exchange systems, parents agree to do something positively valued for the child after the child has done something that the parents value positively. "Since you helped me bring in the groceries, you can have the snack you wanted."
- Using permission systems, parents predicate a freedom on a condition being met. "You can go to the party if you give me the information about arrangements I require."
- Using earning systems, parents attach points to performing desirable behavior, with a certain number of points entitling the child to an agreed-upon reward. "For feeding and cleaning up after the dog each day all week, you earned enough points to get another action figure for your collection."

Negative Systems

Negative systems influence willingness by allowing or applying unwelcome consequences. Used occasion-

ally, these systems can persuade a willful child to cooperate. Parents have to watch out, however, that they are
not too heavy-handed. If you act extremely negative or
highly emotional, a power struggle may ensue. The willful child may be "willing," all right, but not the way
parents want—willing to go down in flames to prove
they can't make him or they can't stop him. Generally,
positive responses have far more power to influence
willingness than negative responses do.

DID YOU KNOW?

Don't use too negative a consequence to threaten a
child. When parents use a fearful consequence such
as dire threat or physical hurt to motivate willingness,
the child may go along with what they want, but at
considerable expense to the relationship. The cost
of coercion is loss of trust, loss of honesty, loss of
closeness, and, in extreme situations, loss of love.

Negative choice/consequence connections include
the following:

- Using accountability systems, parents hold the
  child responsible for coping with unhappy
  consequences of poor decisions. "You have to
  clean up what you spilled."
- Using warning systems, parents promise the
  child what consequence will happen if timely
  compliance is not given. "I'm going to count
  to three, and if by three you have not started

to get ready, I will follow through with what I
promised."

- Using penalty systems, parents attach a negative
  consequence of their choosing to discourage repetition of a misbehavior. "For lying to me, there
  is going to be some more work for you to do
  around here in addition to your normal chores."

Subverting Cooperation—and How to Deal with It

When a child is in a position of unwillingness, ignoring or resisting your demands, first remind yourself that
you have no control over the child's behavior. This is
not a problem to try and change. It is a very important
reality to accept.

The loss of control for parents to be concerned about
is not over their child, but over themselves. They can
subvert cooperation they want by losing control of their
own behavior in two common ways. First, they may
emotionally load a situation by overreacting to a child's
resistance and end up intensifying an encounter better
handled by a cooler head and a more reasoned approach.
Or, they can repeat unproductive choices because they
cannot think of what else to do. In both cases, they have
lost control over their own effective decision making,
reducing the likelihood that they will be given the willingness they want.

DID YOU KNOW?

When parents believe they can control their willful child's decision making, they are in danger of

losing control by trying to force control, at which point the child ends up in control by demonstrating how powerless the parents actually are. "I don't care how mean you act or angry you get, the more you punish, the more I'll fail!"

Emotional Loading

Emotional loading occurs when parents choose to apply inflammatory labels or inflammatory interpretations to their child's behavior, offending the child and upsetting the parents in the process.

How can parents emotionally load a child's problem? "All I did was not turn in some homework and fail a test and my mom got really scared, my dad got really angry, and we had this big fight. 'Do you want to be a failure in life?' they yelled. I never knew I could get them so upset just by making a few bad grades!" And then the willful child, injured by their label and incited by their upset, decides to get back at parents for the insult by deliberately failing again.

The lesson is, if you want cooperation in resolving a significant issue with your willful child, do not load up the issue with emotion. Exploding and yelling at your child to go to bed on time, to stay in bed, to go to sleep, will not get you the cooperation you desire. It will increase the unwillingness you do not want by emotionally inflaming an ordinary disagreement. So get a grip on yourself. Do whatever you must to restore a rational state of mind. Think about what different choices you could make in your own behavior to influence your child to go along with what you'd like. The less emotional parents remain when working a problem through with their willful child, the more likely they are to get the cooperation they desire. "Here's a clock. I want you to try staying in bed for an hour, and if you still can't get to sleep by then, I want you to come in and tell me so we can try again."

Repeating Unproductive Choices

"Nothing works!" protest the parents. "There's nothing left to do!" Parents may give up exploring new ways of behaving with the child to encourage a more timely bedtime, for example. And instead, they keep repeating unproductive choices that recent history has shown have failed. They cajole, they plead, they bargain, they get angry, they make threats, and night after night the war over bedtime is reenacted to predictable, dispiriting, and exhausting effect. Repeating choices that have proven ineffective will not get parents the cooperation they desire.

"But we've tried everything!" they argue. This is the wrong attitude. Parents have never "tried everything," because there an infinite number of experimental approaches and responses for them to try. What parents have run out of is the will to try, to keep thinking up new choices for influencing their child. Three techniques for breaking out of this inability to come up with new ideas are violating the child's prediction, enlisting the child in the problem solving, and brainstorming with a friend.

Violate the Child's Prediction

Ask yourself, "How does my child predict I will act when this problem comes up again?" Perhaps you answer, "When he delays going to bed on time, he probably predicts that I will disagree with his excuse and begin an argument." So surprise him. Agree with his excuse. Compliment his excuse. Tell him you'd like to hear other good excuses, and you'll be lying down on his bed when he wants to come in and tell you some more. Who knows, it might work.

Enlist the Child in the Problem Solving

Instead of treating bedtime resistance as just your problem, understand that the nightly fights are probably also a problem for your child. So, during a relaxed morning time, ask your child what he thinks might work to make bedtime go more smoothly. He may have some ideas of his own. "Well, I'd like us to have a friendly way of going to bed. Just you and me, maybe playing a game after I'm all ready so we can have some fun together." Who knows, it might work.

Brainstorm with a Friend

Ask a friend to work with you to come up with twenty crazy ideas for getting your child to bed on time. No objections to any of the ideas allowed. Try reversing things. Take bedtime away from him. Treat it as a privilege, not an obligation. Tell him, 'Tonight you can't go to bed until we think you have earned it. We have three jobs you have to do before you can lie down and read yourself to sleep.'" Who knows, it might work.

DOES THIS SOUND LIKE YOUR CHILD?

Just because a child is strong-willed does not mean that all refusals to cooperate are deliberate acts of willful opposition. Sometimes parents have unrealistic expectations of the child's capacity to perform (for example, she does not like playing on a more competitive team). Sometimes parents demand faster adjustment to change than the child has the immediate adaptive capacity to easily make (for example, he complains about living in a new place and attending a new school). In either case, at the moment, resistance signifies the child can do no more.

With a willful child, parents must keep generating new and different choices for influencing his behavior. Gaining cooperation depends on parents never running out of new options to try.

Chapter 5

Who's Running Your Family?

Ten Things You Will Learn in This Chapter

- How to figure out who's really in charge of your family.

- That being trapped in your preoccupation of your child can really hurt your family.

- How to avoid neglecting your other children!

- How to avoid straining your marriage when parenting you strong-willed child.

- What positive responsiveness is and how it's your strongest tool!

- What the first step to correct a persistent problem is.

- To avoid becoming disorganized and scattered—and why this is so important.

- Four lessons you should concentrate on each day to better your child's behavior.

- How to keep self-consciousness and responsibility.

- About reactive and proactive methods of parenting—and which will suit your child the best.

Where's Your Sense of Priority?

For many parents there are times when power becomes reversed, and instead of the parents being in charge, it seems as if the strong-willed child is running the family. They constantly react to her impulses and respond to her ultimatums. They keep waiting to see what kind of mood she's in, stay worried about her becoming upset, and continually endeavor to keep her happy. They struggle to get her compliance, trying to convince her to make cooperative choices. They strive to establish a family structure into which she will fit and to set a family agenda she will agree to follow. This chapter describes some of the telltale changes in parental behavior that signal the presence of a child in the family who has too much power for everyone's good.

DID YOU KNOW?

One risk of parenting a strong-willed child is neglecting other siblings. Parents must not become so absorbed in coping with the demands of their strong-willed child that they ignore the less urgent (but every bit as important) needs for attention of other children in the family.

When a willful child is allowed to rule the family, parents primarily focus on problems posed by the child's dominant behavior and ignore what should be higher priorities. Overwhelmed by concern for the child, parents think and talk of little else. They set everything else aside to focus on the child, soon feeling trapped by the child, usually growing angry on that account. Undue self-sacrifice often begets resentment.

Actually, they are not trapped by the child. They are trapped by their preoccupation with the child and what that preoccupation has caused them to give up. Now they begin to blame the child for what lack of adequate self-care and lack of marital care are starting to cost—stress on each of them and erosion of the marriage relationship. "You're driving us crazy and ruining our marriage with all the conflict you cause between us!" No. The parents are electing to drive themselves crazy and to neglect the marriage on the child's behalf.

There are certain functional priorities that a healthy family should have. The first priority is for both parents to take adequate care of their individual selves so that each has sufficient energy and positive attention to devote to other members of the family. The second priority (if there are two parents in the home) is to take sufficient care of the marriage so their partnership is nourished and their parenting remains united. And the third priority is taking care of the children's needs and wants.

By elevating the willful child to number one, the boy or girl is inappropriately empowered, parental energy gets run down, and the marriage becomes more estranged and conflicted from lack of adequate attention. Take good care of yourselves first and your marriage second, and healthy family functioning, upon which the child's welfare ultimately depends, tends to follow. Continually treat the willful child as the first priority, and the child will only become more willful, expecting and demanding to be treated as number one in a family that increasingly centers on his wants and needs. To take good care of your children, put them last.

DID YOU KNOW?

Parents frequently set aside their needs to attend to those of their child. The child is best served when the individual and marital needs of parents are taken care of first. Stressed, divided parents are hard-pressed to create a stable and supportive consistent family structure on which their child can securely depend.

Seeing Nothing but the Negative

The most telling, and the most damaging, characteristic of parents who are ruled by a strong-willed child is an overwhelming negative attitude toward that boy or girl. This negativity has massive ill effect. Consider the following examples:

- It discourages the child from making efforts to self-correct, because there is nothing positive to work for in the relationship. "All you ever do is get angry, threaten, criticize, or punish, so why should I do what you want?"
- It discourages the child, who comes to see himself fitting the terms parents describe. "My parents say I'm nothing but trouble. They're right, I am!"
- It discourages parents because the more negative they feel, the more negative they act, and the

more negative their willful child usually acts in
response. "The more we punish, the more determined she becomes not to do what we ask!"

- It discourages parental self-esteem because as the
parents grow more negative toward their child,
they grow more negative toward themselves.
"We're just lousy parents; that's the bottom line!"

This negativity can be extremely destructive. It can
cause a loss of positive perspective. What both parents
and child need at this point is to be pumped up with
positive regard. When parents cease to recognize and
reward the good in their willful child's behavior, they
end up losing the greatest power of influence they
have—positive responsiveness. Where negative parental
outlook and behavior are the rule, the willful child is
usually in charge.

It is the responsibility of parents to keep the broadest
possible picture of their child so that any problem that
arises is kept in a larger perspective. Unhappily, embat-
tled parents of a strong-willed child often cannot see the
forest for the trees. They can't see all that is going well
because they are so focused on what is going wrong.

Particularly when the willful child's choice seems
self-defeating (falling grades from not completing some
homework) or potentially self-destructive (engaging in
periodic substance use), parents may equate the problem with the person, even though the willful child protests against this restrictive and unrealistic identification. "Bad grades are not all I am!" "Using pot is not
all I do!"

The first step parents need to take when working with their child to help correct a persistent problem is to inventory everything else that is going well, to appreciate all the good choices the child is making and all the bad choices that he's not making. "Your attendance, class work, and test scores are good; it's just not doing homework that is bringing your grades down." "You're taking care of business at school, you're driving responsibly, you're holding down a part-time job, you help out and do your chores at home, you do so much that we appreciate. It's just that your smoking pot on some weekends with friends is causing us concern."

DOES THIS SOUND LIKE YOUR CHILD?

When a willful child makes wrong-headed choices, parents must remember that any problem is a small part of a large person who performs well in other areas of life. Without this larger perspective, both parents and child are at risk of ignoring positive functioning and personal strengths that could otherwise be helpfully called into play.

Are You Scattered and Distracted?

When a willful child is allowed to rule the family, parents become increasingly disorganized in the structure and discipline they provide. This disorganization only creates more freedom for their child. The more disorganized and scattered they are, the more confused they become, the more they lose touch with their parenting priorities. The more distracted they are, the more inconsistent and ineffective their discipline becomes. In both cases, the willful child gains more ruling power.

DID YOU KNOW?

Parents must keep their larger training objectives clearly in mind and not allow themselves to become scattered by the multiplicity and intensity of the willful child's demands. When they get lost in coping moment to moment, they will lose touch with larger parenting priorities, and the willful child will only gather more power.

Scattered Attention

When a willful child rules the family, urgently pushing here and intensively resisting there, parents can move into crisis management mode, just coping with incidents and outbursts as they occur. Parenting moment to moment in this way, their attention becomes scattered as they try to cope with the latest outburst or incident at the expense of sustaining important child-raising priorities. "Sure, we know teaching him habits of picking up after himself, asking for instead of taking what he wants, and following rules for safety are all important, but when he's always running off for freedom or throwing tantrums when we say no, we forget the bigger picture for the small."

Living in chaos is confusing. It's hard to keep your focus. It's hard to remember training issues that matter most. It's hard to keep a sense of priority. Out of confusion, comes uncertainty about what happened and about what needs to happen. "What did I really say?

I can't remember." "What should I do? I can't decide." The outcome of uncertainty, begotten by confusion from crisis management, is hit-or-miss parenting—just doing something, anything, to respond to the moment. The willful child is definitely in charge.

It may seem artificial, but it is worth writing down your priorities. To keep clarity about your parenting priorities, and to not fall prey to confusion from becoming scattered, post a list of your most important objectives where you can see it each day. For example, "Our priorities each day are to:

1. Teach our child to speak in respectful and not hurtful language
2. Teach our child not to hit or take
3. Teach our child to stop and listen when we speak
4. Teach our child to fit into the family schedule."

A written reminder can refocus attention.

Becoming Distracted

It takes consistency to maintain discipline, to train a child to live within family rules and to act according to family values. Because a willful child can test parental tolerances and contest their authority on so many fronts, it is easy for parents to be distracted from attending to one issue when the child raises another—a strategy willful adolescents use all the time.

"I was in the process of checking to see if homework had been taken care of when she began arguing about her right to privacy. Then, when I shifted focus to address the issue of privacy, she turned on the TV, which she knows is against the rules until after her homework is done!" Push, push, push! Keeping parents in a continual state of distraction is one way a willful child comes to rule the family. It's not that discipline breaks down so much as that it is never given enough consistency of application to take hold. In this case, the parent should have stuck to supervising homework and ignored other distractions until the checking was complete. No matter the distractions, deal with one issue at a time.

DOES THIS SOUND LIKE YOUR CHILD?

The willful child can use distraction to encourage parental inconsistency, repeatedly pushing against limits parents have not firmly set, repeatedly disobeying rules that parents only selectively enforce, and repeatedly putting off demands that parents easily forget. Be persistent and consistent!

Focusing on What You Can't Control

When a willful child is allowed to rule the family, parents suffer two common losses: loss of self-consciousness and loss of responsibility. In each case, they focus on what they can't control at the expense of attending to what they can.

Loss of Self-Consciousness

Consider the parents who are in constant struggle to put their willful child to bed on time. They're very clear about where the problem lies: "It's her bedtime behavior that's causing all the trouble. She refuses to stay put. She's always getting up to ask for one more thing. It's infuriating! But no matter how angry we get, she fights us every night until she's finally so exhausted she falls asleep. By then, we're so tired from the struggle, we end up bickering between ourselves!"

By placing the problem on the child's behavior (which they don't control), the parents have lost focus on their own (which they do control). What's going on here is an interaction between parents and child at bedtime that is resulting in the child's refusing to stay in bed. Perhaps, if they would focus on their own conduct, they might identify some changes in themselves that might make a difference. For example, instead of acting angry and unloving, which may cause the child to act frightened and cling for additional parental contact, putting off dreaded time alone, they might want to create a playful ritual that would help bedtime feel welcome, peaceful, and secure.

It is tempting for parents to get so preoccupied with what their willful child is doing "wrong" or isn't doing "right" that they lose self-consciousness of their own behavior and their influential role in the interaction. In this case, when parents identify the bedtime problem as partly their own, they can choose to act differently to encourage a different response from their child.

Loss of Responsibility
Good advice for parents of a willful child is "Don't play the blame game." Overwhelmed by insistent

demand and stubborn refusal, parents can get fed up and run down, venting their displeasure by blaming the child for their unhappy state. "Of course we're irritable. It's all our daughter's fault! If she weren't so obstinate and demanding, we wouldn't be so cranky!"

Blame casts off responsibility, empowering the person blamed and victimizing the blamer. When a willful child is allowed to rule the family, parents usually concede this domination through casting blame.

Reactive Instead of Proactive

When a willful child is allowed to rule the family, parents are on the reactive too much of the time. Of course, when a child is born, parents are immediately put on the reactive. They respond when discontent and distress are expressed, they try to figure out what the infant wants and needs, and they often feel the little child is calling the shots as they adjust to the fussing, feeding, playing, and sleeping pattern of this newcomer in the family. As the child grows older, parents are gradually able to conform the boy's or girl's schedule to better suit their own, and the child is increasingly reactive to demands of the parents.

When the child is by nature or nurture strong-willed, however, parents can remain on the reactive and get in the habit of putting their own initiatives on hold, waiting to see what their willful child wants or does before deciding how to act. When this habit of parental reactivity takes shape, they have given that child too much ruling power. "We rarely make family plans anymore because we don't know what kind of mood he'll be in or how he'll act. Mostly we base what we do on what he's done, is willing to do, or will do next. A lot of times it's easier to let him lead the way."

Taking Initiative

Willful children are more demanding to live with in two ways. They literally tend to make more demands than other children do, and they are more intense about the demands they make. In the face of the rate and intensity of these demands, it is understandable that parents would become focused on responding to what the child wants and doesn't want to do.

To take back initiative with their willful child, parents have to bravely become more demanding in the relationship. They have to put their child back on the reactive. For example, consider the prickly fourteen-year-old who is currently ruling the family. "She's always arguing and up for a fight at the slightest question we ask or request we make, and gets really impatient with us when we don't do what she wants right away. So for the sake of peace and quiet, we've learned to tiptoe around her bad moods, which are most of the time, and approach her just when she seems approachable, which isn't very often. We can usually tell how bad her day has been by how hard she slams the front door when she gets home and by how quickly she storms off to her room to be left alone."

How can parents take back the initiative? They can greet her at the door with questions and demands, and when she tries to back them off, they can brush her intensity and objections aside in determined pursuit of the information they want and the tasks they need accomplished. Often some conflict is provoked for parents when they move to take initiative back, but if they are resolved to show they mean business, if they don't back off or back down, and if they keep up their demands, the child will come around. She will grudgingly accept that, when it comes to interaction in the family, parents are going to initiate the most demands.

A BETTER PARENTING PRACTICE

Although parents should hold the willful child responsible for choices he makes (and for facing the consequences), they must be careful not to shift responsibility for their feelings to the child through blame: "Our unhappiness is all our child's fault!" By victimizing themselves, they arm the child with the belief that he is in charge of their well-being.

Setting the Agenda

What happens when the child begins to increasingly set the agenda for the family? As parents become more reactive to the child, their loss of influence is the child's gain. "I want us to go out to eat tonight!" declares the child to parents who had been planning for them all to eat at home. Then they explain and she complains. They become firm. She starts to whine and soon becomes upset. They begin to waver. Now she sweetens up to soften them up. And finally, to avoid a tiring conflict at the end of a long day, they let her have her way. The child's agenda has prevailed.

Taking back control of the family agenda requires proactive parenting. Parents have to plan what they want to have happen, declare that plan to the child, and stick to that plan even when the child objects. To get control of the family agenda back where it belongs, parents can start each day informing the child about the schedule of planned events and arrangements that have been made. Certainly they can ask for the child's input to better encourage his cooperation, but the main point that preplanning makes is that the parents, not the child, are in charge of organizing the flow of family events.

Chapter 6

How to Get Back in Charge

Ten Things You Will Learn in This Chapter

- What to say and how to say it to regain control.
- About certain communication tactics that don't work!
- About the communication tactics that absolutely work!
- How to clarify responsibilities without giving away too much power.
- To watch out for willful promises and how to react to them.
- How to avoid appropriating too much responsibility.
- How to find the positive consent in your child's actions and use this to the best of your abilities.
- About the two criteria for parental authority.
- Some assertive actions you can take to communicate corrective authority.
- How to nicely but effectively discipline your child.

Work on Communication

Because it is neither responsible nor healthy for a willful child to be allowed to rule the family, parents must do what they can to get back in charge. But what can they do? There are some building blocks that must be put back in place to restore parental influence. They have to do with clearing up communication, resetting boundaries of responsibility, assessing consent, asserting authority, and keeping a positive perspective.

DID YOU KNOW?

It's not what hardships parents and willful child go through with each other that count most in their long-term relationship; it's how they go through them. And the key to that "how" is communication. Parents and children who openly and effectively communicate through turbulent times end up closely connected. Those who do not, end up estranged.

By the time a willful child has come to rule the family, parental communication with that child has usually fallen into considerable disarray. What they say and how they say it often incite the child to become more entrenched in acting in ways they do not want. Since verbal communication is chosen behavior, not genetic or fixed, parents can change the tone and content of their speech. If they know what not to do, they can stop doing that. If they know what to do, they can start doing that.

Communication That Doesn't Work

Here are some don'ts to consider:

- **Don't be critical.** Willful children are extremely sensitive to criticism. Because they get so much of it, they are on guard against it. Rather than receive what you have to say, they will block it out or fight you back.

- **Don't be emotional.** Willful children are already intense. Adding your own emotion, particularly when in existing conflict, only arouses more emotion in the child.

- **Don't be abstract.** Using vague or general terms ("You are lazy, messy, and irresponsible") to express your disagreement only communicates disapproval without clarifying specific charges that are causing you offense. "You are a day late taking your belongings out of the living room as you promised."

- **Don't be inconsistent.** Selective enforcement of significant rules only communicates that some-times you mean business and sometimes you do not. Given this mixed message, the willful child will gamble that you don't.

- **Don't be locked in.** Don't stick to disciplin-ary decisions that don't work only because you are too tired to think of anything else—this only demonstrates how bankrupt of influential choices you have become. You must keep trying something different until something works—for a while.

- **Don't be impatient.** Most willful children are already too impatient for their own good. Don't encourage this trait by modeling impatience of your own. Impatience only speeds up a sense of urgency and empowers impulse when both parent and child would be better served by more deliberate decision making that slows down intensity.

- **Don't get distracted.** Stick to the issue at hand until it is settled, and don't let your child shift the focus to something else. Distraction is the enemy of resolution. Distraction favors your willful child by throwing you off the subject of discussion.

- **Don't be negative.** The more negative you become, the less willingness—cooperation and consent—you will motivate in your child.

- **Don't be accusatory.** The more you attack your willful child for not doing what you want, the more defensive he or she is likely to become, and the more counterattack will ignite conflict between you.

- **Don't use extremes.** Better not to use "You always" or "You never" in describing misbehavior, because such statements deny or discount those times when willingness you want has been given. "You never do what you're asked!" may feel emotionally true, but it is factually false. You want to be sure to reward with recognition every act of cooperation your child gives you.

Communication That Does Work

Here are some do's to consider.

- **Do be nonevaluative.** When disciplining, remember that, for your willful child, correction is criticism enough. Any additional judgment is only likely to arouse more resistance. So when some misbehavior has occurred, say, "We disagree with the choice you have made, here is why, and this is what we need to have happen in consequence."

- **Do be reasonable.** When you model the use of reason in disagreement, and do not resort to emotion, your example encourages the child to adopt a reasonable approach in response. Explain why you want what you want, and then try to negotiate an agreement.

- **Do be operational.** When describing what you want or do not want your child doing, talk contractually in terms of specific behaviors and events. "What I need to have happen is for you to be home by the curfew time on which we agreed."

- **Do be consistent.** If you want to train your child to follow your rules, then you must faithfully articulate and enforce those rules so your habit of consistency encourages a consistent habit of compliance in response.

- **Do be resourceful.** Keep thinking up new approaches for influencing your child when old ones lose their persuasive power. If your child

knows you will never run out of choices, then he
or she knows you will never give up.

A BETTER PARENTING PRACTICE

Quality of family life largely depends on the quality of communication between family members. The
job of parents is to model the kind of communication they want their children to use and to monitor
everyone's communication so that spoken language
remains respectful and hurts no one.

- **Do be patient.** Don't get upset or give up if
  you don't get your way with your willful child
  right away. Just act like you have all the time
  and energy it takes to keep insisting until your
  request is met. The message patience sends is "I
  will not be defeated by delay."
- **Do stay focused.** Keep your mind on what matters most. If you don't stick to your parenting
  priorities, then your child won't either.
- **Do be empathetic.** Show your child that no
  matter how you may disagree with his or her
  actions, your first concern is with how the child
  feels. "Before we deal with what happened, I
  want to hear about what caused you to feel so
  upset."
- **Do be moderate.** Extreme statements and measures by parents tend to provoke extreme statements and measures in response from the willful
  child. To keep interactions on an even keel,

follow the middle way. "A lot of times you do, sometimes you don't, and this time you didn't."

Clarify Responsibilities

To get back in charge, parents must be clear about what they are in charge of and what they are not in charge of. Simply put, they are responsible for only their own decision making. They are not responsible for the decision making of their child any more than the child is responsible for the decision making of the parents. This means that parents must beware two kinds of boundary errors that end up only empowering the willful child in unhealthy ways.

In the first error, they strengthen the child's position by blaming the child for abusing responsibility they have given him or her. In the second error, they strengthen the child's position by blaming themselves for what the child is actually responsible for.

Giving Away Too Much Responsibility

Beware the willful promise. When a willful child wants something very much, he or she will make all kinds of extreme promises to get parents to give permission or to relent.

- "If you get me the puppy, I promise I'll do all the care and you won't have to remind me or do any yourselves!"
- "If you let me go to the party tonight, I promise I'll stay home the next month of weekends and help around the place with no complaints!"

- "If you get me shoes like my friends have, I promise I'll do my chores without having to be nagged!"

Willful promises can sound very convincing; that's why parents are so easily taken in. In most cases, the child promises to take some kind of responsibility in exchange for what he seeks. In many cases, however, the willful child lacks sufficient power of responsibility to keep the promises he or she makes. So parents end up with most of the caretaking of the puppy, having to argue to keep the child at home on the weekends as agreed, or pursuing the completion of chores.

Parents err in giving in to promises of responsibility the child is not prepared to keep. From past experience, parents recognize that their child won't keep her word, but they keep taking it anyway because she is so convincing that they think she means it at the time. Parental hope can be a great denier and deceiver.

Appropriating Too Much Responsibility

When parents believe that they are in charge of the child's decisions, they take over responsibility that properly belongs to the child. "It's our fault that she started experimenting with drugs. If we hadn't gotten divorced, this never would have happened!" No, their daughter is electing to experiment with drugs. If she is using substances to cope with unhappy feelings stemming from parental divorce, she needs to know and own that she has other choices for managing her unhappiness. The more parents blame themselves, the more their daughter will deny responsibility, casting it off onto them. Parental guilt can be a great enabler, children gathering unhealthy power of irresponsibility by exploiting parental self-blame.

A BETTER PARENTING PRACTICE

To get back in charge after a willful child has come to rule the family, parents must clearly and consistently observe appropriate boundaries of responsibility—neither blaming their child for their own decisions nor blaming themselves for the child's decisions.

Do You Have Consent—Is It Even Enough?

In the extremity of their frustration, anger, and helplessness with a child who is ruling the family, parents' perceptions of what is going on can become distorted. "She never does anything we want, only what she wants!" This statement is both false and true. It is false because she sometimes does do what they want. It is true because the child, like anybody else, only does what she wants to do, even when she doesn't like doing whatever that is.

The first part of the statement can do a lot of damage. If they truly believe she never does anything they want, then they will feel totally defied, and the child will not get recognition or credit for the compliance she sometimes gives. In truth, no child is 100 percent defiant, no matter how it may feel to the parents, and no parents are totally without influence. To some degree, some of the time, even the most recalcitrant child is cooperative. Call this willingness to go along *consent*.

To get back in charge, parents need to recognize and affirm that all is not lost. Although their willful child seems to be ruling the family, a lot of the time he is giving them consent of two kinds: doing what they want him to do, and not doing what they don't want him to do.

Identifying Positive Consent

Take a time out and list out all the things the child is doing that you want him to do. He may be a fussy eater, but he is eating. He may not be doing much homework, but he is going to school and doing class work there. He may sometimes use rude language to you, but he is polite to adults who come over and to adults away from family. He may be breaking some home rules, but he is following rules at school and social laws. The point is, you are not bankrupt of influence. You are just not having as much influence and getting as much cooperation as you would like.

Identifying Negative Consent

Next, list out all the things you can think of that he is not doing that you don't want him to do and have told him not to do. The world is full of dangerous and forbidden possibilities open to your child, and you can't change the world. More than that, you are operating a home, not a prison. The child could experiment in all kinds of ways but is not. Why not? Only his choices are keeping him from trying out these negative possibilities. So when assessing consent, credit the child for the dangerous risks and forbidden temptations he is resisting. For example, although she sometimes comes in after curfew, she is not late for school. Although she sometimes borrows her mother's clothes without asking, she does not shoplift from stores. Although she hangs out with friends who smoke, she is not smoking herself.

A BETTER PARENTING PRACTICE

When parents are in the process of getting back in charge, they should identify and appreciate the positive and negative consent they are being given, because that is the base on which more consent can be built.

Assert Your Authority

A willful child cannot come to rule the family unless parents have backed off due to relentless demands and determined resistance over a sustained period of time. For parents to get back in charge, they must establish or reclaim authority.

There are two criteria for parental authority: parents must say what they mean and mean what they say. "Before you get to play with friends on Saturday, all your weekend chores must be completed." If words fail to convince, parents back up their words with actions to show they mean business. "I'm not driving you over to your friend's until your chores are done."

When a willful child is allowed to rule the family, he or she has learned "don't" and "won't"—that parents don't mean what they say and won't back up what they say with actions. "So what authority is there to respect?" thinks the child. And at the moment, the answer is "not much," since parents caved in to her complaints once again, letting her go without chores accomplished, just as they did last weekend. Rules without enforcement earn no respect. Two kinds of authority need to be restored: corrective authority, which asserts parental influence the child dislikes, and contributive authority, which demonstrates parental powers that the child values receiving.

Corrective Authority

There are many assertive acts through which parents communicate corrective authority. Consider just a few:

- Requesting information
- Holding accountable
- Asking questions
- Confronting issues
- Checking performance
- Giving directions
- Setting conditions
- Applying consequences
- Advising choices
- Stating prohibitions
- Maintaining supervision
- Making judgments
- Stating expectations
- Enforcing rules

Through these and other corrective acts, you establish authoritative standing with the child. When you start practicing these acts, you can create or reclaim an authoritative presence in the child's life—so long as you mean what you say and are committed to backing up your words with actions if it's required to convince your child that you are serious. When words alone don't work, you must take action to show you mean business.

Contributive Authority

An equally powerful source of authority, which the willful child may take for granted because demanding makes it so easy to get, is contributive authority—acts that demonstrate how parental authority can benefit the child. Parents have the power to do many things for the child that the child, no matter how willful, is unable to do for herself. When children experience and appreciate what parental authority is good for ("My parents can help me figure out my homework when I get stuck"), they realize that it is not all bad. Consider just a few of the ways contributive parental authority can be of use:

- For protection
- For advocacy
- For getting help
- For encouragement
- For approval
- For support
- For instruction
- For problem solving
- For providing permission
- For releasing resources

So, when going through a parental passage that requires more corrective authority, be sure you find ways to mix into this negative period some times when contributive authority comes into play. "I know I'm on your case a lot to get off the phone to get your school work done, so let's take a break from the supervision and arguments and go out for something to eat." The more you rely on corrective authority, the more you need to maintain acts of contributive authority so your "bad" influence is leavened by the "good."

Now, Stay Positive!

Probably the hardest challenge when parenting a willful child is maintaining a positive attitude in the face of stubborn self-determination and ongoing resistance. Parents' sense of effectiveness can be eroded to the point that they feel frustrated and helpless a lot of the time, and they may feel angry on that account.

Anger is an inherently critical emotion. It responds to perceived violations of one's well-being. "This is wrong. This is unfair. This shouldn't happen. This is not what I want. This isn't right." Anger also empowers an expressive, protective, or corrective response. Under the influence of anger, parents can make the situation with their child worse by allowing themselves to become excessively negative and insufficiently positive.

The High Cost of Negativity

"After a while we get tired of the constant struggle for compliance and we just wear down," parents confess. And with the use of the term "wear down," they announce the other cause for their discouraged state of mind. They are exhausted and they are fatigued. Fatigue can act like a mood- and mind-altering chemical that casts a pall of negativity over perception and motivation. "It's all going downhill; there's no point in trying." From chronic negativity grows pessimism.

Negativity lies. It keeps you from recognizing the intermittent consent and cooperation the child gives, and makes you feel like giving up when what's really necessary is keeping on. On the receiving end of this stream of negativity, the child becomes discouraged, too, discouraged from working with parents who apparently believe that all he or she is good at is doing bad. So negative parental outlook becomes self-fulfilling as the child decides to act more headstrong and obstinate than ever. "If trouble is all you think I am, then trouble is how I'm going to act!"

The Persuasive Power of the Positive

When parenting a willful child, there is a slogan that is helpful to remember: "No deposit, no return." If you will keep contributing positive responsiveness to your child, even when—particularly when—going through a stormy passage, then your child will see the relationship as having positive personal value and will be more inclined to respond positively to you. If the only attention the child receives from you is in the form of complaint, criticism, and threatened and actual punishment, then you have removed any positive incentive for the child to want to cooperate with you. "There's no pleasing my parents, so why try?"

DID YOU KNOW?

When parenting a willful child, beware negativity. It starts by bringing the parents down, and it ends by bringing the child down. The most effective parents of strong-willed children are those who keep a positive outlook and do not allow hard times to diminish this attitude. Their glass is always half full, never half empty.

Remember that animal trainers do not train animals to do tricks by applying negative reinforcement when the animal fails to perform. Instead, they relentlessly repeat the training exercise, always rewarding effort to keep up the creature's will to try, and rewarding desired outcome when it occurs. The same principle applies to gaining cooperation and consent from a willful child. "It's time to practice putting back your toys again. This is hard to learn, and I appreciate your trying. When you get them all put back on your own, we will celebrate!"

Consider every positive response you give your child as putting money in the bank of his or her long-term willingness to cooperate with you. And keep positive and negative (corrective) responses independent of each other. Be negative when you have to, but don't allow the fact that you are going through a prolonged corrective time in pursuit of some behavior change to cause you to diminish the ongoing positive responses you invest in his willingness to work with you.

A BETTER PARENTING PRACTICE

To keep from becoming unduly negative with your willful child, practice the rule of two for one. For every negative or corrective response you make, within the next hour find an authentic way to make two positive responses to show how you value the child and appreciate his or her efforts.

When parents assume authority ("We are in charge because we are the parents"), when they clearly define the family rules ("This is what you can and cannot do"), when they expect compliance ("We know you will behave as you've been taught"), and when they consistently reward consent and correct infractions ("This response is in consequence for what you did"), they will re-establish their leadership role within the family.

Chapter 7

Bumps on the Road to Regaining Control

Ten Things You Will Learn in This Chapter

- What an intractable child is and find out if you have one!

- What it takes to change your child's habits.

- Practical ways to clarify structure—like writing out a list of rules.

- How to state your rules in a way that will work!

- What the most common failure in parental discipline is.

- What to do when your child becomes violent.

- How your child's anger may be hiding some underlying issues.

- How to teach your child self-awareness.

- About secrecy and it's link to family violence.

- How to recognize warning signs and help a suicidal child before it's too late.

The Intractable Child

Through demands they make, and how they communicate those demands, parents can get back in charge.
In the case of the intractable child, this requires clear,
concerted, consistent, and changed parental effort over
time to gradually retrain the willful child to accept a
more appropriate and subordinate role in the family. What parental words have failed to convey, now
actions must be taken to convince. In the case of the
violent child, this requires willingness to confront the
child in a variety of ways to encourage nonviolent
choices for managing hard feelings and urgent wants.
In both cases, parents have to alter their behavior to
encourage resumption of acceptable conduct by their
willful child.

The intractable child is one whose determined willfulness makes him extremely difficult to govern, to the
point that parents often feel it is the child who is running the family and not themselves. Parents typically
feel frustrated, angry, and helpless; are negatively dis-
posed toward the child a lot of the time; feel bad about
themselves; and have lost the ability to establish structure and assert authority the child will respect.

It is much easier to give a child power than it is to
take it back, and the intractable willful child who is now
calling the shots has little incentive to give up the freedom of choice and unbridled influence he has gained.
The intractable child poses an ongoing problem for parents, not an occasional one. They find themselves on the
losing side of a daily struggle about who is going to live
on whose terms—the child on their terms, or they on

the child's terms. The intractable child is accustomed to being in charge.

A BETTER PARENTING PRACTICE

You may wonder what kinds of demands should parents make when taking back the initiative. Asking for household help is a good place to start because that request subordinates what the child wants to do to serving someone else. The underlying message is, "There are other needs in the family more important than your own."

Consider parents with an intractable eight-year-old who, among other acts of willfulness:

- Eats snacks when he wants to and doesn't eat meals when he doesn't want to
- Refuses to pick up after himself
- Won't do household chores
- Uses hurtful name-calling when angry
- Takes siblings' belongings when he wants to use them
- Won't come along when parents ask
- Throws tantrums when parents deny him what he wants
- Routinely puts off homework so it rarely gets done

The intractable child has learned habits of willful behavior that retraining will not change overnight. It takes teaching new habits to replace old habits, and that takes time. Commit to the effort such retraining takes, and by the end, you will still have a willful child, but one who goes along more with what you want than he did before.

What's Your Goal?

With retraining, you must recognize that your goal is to change habits—patterns of behavior learned through repetition over time until they have become automatic—not to break old habits. You must do this not just by discouraging the old behavior with an unhappy consequence, but by teaching the child a new way to manage frustration, positively rewarding each incident of changed behavior often enough so that a new, more constructive habit is gradually established. The rewards parents use need to be relational, not material, giving the child appreciation, approval, affection, or praise each time he shows improvement.

"But we're not getting anywhere!" complain the parents. "We went two weeks without her name-calling and thought progress was being made, and then last night she exploded into profanity again, so now we're back to where we started!" Not true. Notice what the parents are doing here. They are discounting two weeks of progress for one incident of regress. They discredit the good and credit the bad because of the negative mindset they have established.

In fact, parents should have been letting the child know all those two weeks how they appreciate the changed use of language when frustration has occurred.

And when the name-calling recurred, they should have let the child know that now this is the exception, not the rule, and that they are aware of that. The goal of recovering from harmful habits is "progress, not perfection."

If you truly aren't making any progress, or things are getting worse, then you might need professional help for your child. An evaluation by your pediatrician, a child psychologist, or even a child psychiatrist can be helpful for these strong-willed children.

How to Retrain the Intractable Child

It takes clarity of structure, commitment to priorities, consistency of supervision, connecting choice and consequence, and constancy of affirmation for parents to retrain the child to accept more cooperative family living and to get their working authority back. Retraining takes concerted effort and considerable time. It is not a quick and easy fix.

DID YOU KNOW?

Lack of consistency is the most common failure in parental discipline. Inconsistent discipline keeps parenting from being effective.

Clarifying Structure

The opening step in retraining your freedom-loving child is to clarify the basic parental rules that children in the family are expected to follow. Write out on large paper the five or ten most important rules, explain them to your child, and post this paper in a conspicuous place where it can catch his attention daily. State the rules specifically, not abstractly. Not, "Treat each family member respectfully," but "Ask and be given permission before using another family member's belongings."

Each morning before or after breakfast for the next three months, or for however long it takes for the child to mostly conform to these rules, you and the child will read them aloud. This exercise is partly to remind the child about the behavior you want, and it is partly to represent your renewed seriousness about having rules followed. This exercise not only clarifies what you expect; it shows that you mean business. The specific written statement has symbolic value: the child has been put on notice that you have changed.

Committing to Priorities

The intractable child is usually acting out of parental bounds in so many areas that it's hard for parents to know where retraining should begin. If they try to change everything at once (like all eight misbehaviors of the hypothetical intractable child listed earlier) they will end up changing nothing because their efforts will be too scattered to be effective.

Instead, follow the rule of three. At one time, commit to consistently address no more than three behavior areas you'd like to change, and accept that you will only intermittently, as remaining energy permits, keep after the others. This means setting priorities. Which of the eight misbehaviors do parents consider most in need of change? If they select putting an end to hurtful name-calling as the most important, then patrolling that verbal behavior, acting to discourage its occurrence and to encourage nondestructive alternatives, is where they invest their primary attention until their child learns a more constructive habit of communicating frustration. When the new habit seems mostly in place, then they can drop name-calling from their list of priorities and add another.

DID YOU KNOW?

As much as possible, rules should be stated in positive, not negative, terms. Positives tend to elicit cooperation, whereas negatives often inspire opposition. Instead of "Don't fight over what TV programs to watch," write, "Take turns deciding which TV programs are watched." Directions work better than prohibitions with willful children. Do's work better than don'ts. This doesn't mean prohibitions are entirely excluded. "Don't hit, don't steal, don't name-call" do have their place.

Providing Consistent Supervision

When parents swear that they have tried everything to get back in charge, they are mistaken on two counts. First, no parents have tried *everything*, because there are an infinite number of influential choices they could try. Second, and most important, they don't give what they've tried a fair try—repeating it with enough regularity over time to convince the child to finally change behavior in response.

To retrain your intractable child, you must commit to consistency of supervision. If your priority is getting your child to stop using hurtful language when he's frustrated by parental denial, then you must address that expression each and every time it occurs with a corrective response (making amends and doing additional work) until the offending behavior diminishes or ceases. You also need to instructionally provide constructive alternatives and praise the child when one of those alternatives is used. "I really appreciated how you took yourself off to calm down your frustration when I said 'no,' and then afterward talked to me about your disappointment."

A BETTER PARENTING PRACTICE

Removal of any privilege for an infraction should be done matter-of-factly, with no parental criticism or anger. Just make the connection of choice with consequence, and express the hope that tomorrow your child will make more constructive choices so he can enjoy all privileges.

Connecting Choice and Consequence

Time to make a second list to post alongside the list of rules. This second list is of daily privileges the child gets to regularly enjoy at home. Privileges are any valued activities that require parental provision or permission. This list may include having a certain snack food, watching a favorite TV program, playing a video game, shooting hoops in the backyard, instant messaging on the computer, or whatever activities the child likes to get to do.

Then explain, "We want you to get to enjoy your full list of privileges each day, and you can, so long as you follow the rules. That's your choice. Follow the rules and get all your privileges. Break a rule, lose a privilege for that day. If there's no time left that day, then lose a privilege the day after. Choose to follow the rules, and full privileges will be enjoyed for the day. Choose not to follow the rules, and some privilege will be taken away that day. Our wish is that each day you start with full privileges and end up choosing to enjoy them all."

The Violent Child

Willful children may resort to violent actions to assert power and strengthen dominance in the family. Acts of violence may be used to get her way or to protest not getting her way. They may be used to impulsively act out extreme emotion. They can demonstrate inability or unwillingness to abide by the rules that others follow.

Acts of violence are very serious. If they are allowed to continue, the willful child becomes too powerful and dominant for his own and the family's good, and family members feel too threatened and act too intimidated for their own and the child's good. With the willfully violent child, parents must find ways to discourage physically destructive behavior. Hitting, pinching, kicking, biting, hair pulling, threatening harm, throwing or breaking the possessions of others, and the use of abusive language are unsafe behaviors for everyone in the family.

How to Encourage Nonviolent Behavior

Parental confrontation is the key to discouraging violent behavior in willful children. These approaches are listed in rough order of severity and are generally best used in the order in which they are presented here, going to the next level if less powerful confrontations have not had influential effect.

Confronting Feelings

Violent children are usually emotionally upset at the time violence is committed in the family. Anger appears to be the driving force, but it usually is not. Anger commonly acts as a protective cover to conceal more vulnerable feelings hidden underneath—sadness, disappointment, betrayal, jealousy, anxiety, rejection, hurt, frustration, embarrassment, humiliation, or shame, for example.

Bypass the action for the moment to penetrate beneath the anger. You need to empathetically confront the child, not with disapproval or punishment, but with emotional concern, to draw out underlying feelings. "You must be feeling really hurt to act like that. Please tell me what is going on." By empathetically connecting, you can open up emotional disclosure and discuss what is really going on. Immediately after a violent episode is not the time to talk with the child about what happened, why it happened, and any consequence to follow. So long as the child is still emotionally upset, there will be no thinking person home. A parent's first step is helping the child calm feelings down enough so capacity to reason and willingness to discuss are restored.

Violence is acting out strong emotion. Parents want to teach the child to talk out these feelings instead. Turn a destructive act into a constructive discussion about alternative ways to manage whatever unhappiness was going on. Identify any triggering conditions or events that tend to set the child off, like being teased or put down by an older sibling, because there may be mistreatment from others that is involved that needs to be identified and stopped. "I hate it when he calls me fat and stupid!"

Identify and help establish an early self-awareness (warning) system so the child can notice when he or she might be at risk of building to a violent response and so can have a plan in readiness for doing something else. "Next time I start feeling left out or put down by the older kids, I will come and talk to you."

A BETTER PARENTING PRACTICE

Help the violent child understand the emotional damage done by the violent act by reversing roles. "Tell me how it would feel if someone bigger knocked you down and kept hitting on you."

Give an emotional reference to the child that expresses how they feel when such an act of violence takes place. "I feel really sad for the family when any one of us acts to hurt each other." If parents grew up in a family where physical abuse was part of life, they may also want to talk about that. "You know, I grew up in a scary family where violence occurred and people were physically hurt, where it was hard to trust and difficult to love, and so I really want a family of my own that is violence-free."

Confronting the Victim

Having the child confront people who are impacted by his violence can catch the child's attention and cause him to rethink his violent acts. Confronting the victim of violence, the child can hear what it felt like to be on the receiving end of what he did. The victim might say to him, "You threw my favorite toy and broke it, the one I worked to buy with my own money! When you hurt my things, you hurt me!" The child can apologize if he genuinely feels sorry, describing the behavior he is sorry for. If not, ask him to give his idea of how he thinks the victim of his violence felt. "You must have felt angry for what I did." And finally, the child can then be expected to make amends for damage done. "I'll do some work to earn the money to buy you another toy just like it."

Confronting the Consequence of Public Knowledge

In most occasions of family violence, the perpetrator (in this case, the willful child) does not want news of what happened to be broadcast outside of the family because reputation with significant others could be adversely affected. "Don't tell my grandparents!" pleads the child. "I don't want them to know." Make the violent child understand that significant outside others (extended family, close family friends, other important adults) will be told about any act of family violence that he commits. Explain, "When what we have to say is not enough to discourage you from acting this way, then we will reach outside of family to others who care about us for advice on what we can do." The child learns that private family acts of violence will receive public attention, that attention affecting his or her reputation.

One of the most powerful responses parents can make when a willful child engages in family violence is to "let in the eyes of the world" by letting significant others outside the family know what has happened, soliciting their advice, and letting the child know his violent act has become more widely known. Secrecy only enables family violence.

Confronting Concerned Others

If the previous confrontations have failed to persuade the willful child to cease his violent ways, assemble a circle of caring. To his surprise, the child finds a circle of significant adults assembled at home, all of whom are there to express caring and support for him. Include a grandparent, an aunt, an uncle, a couple of close family friends, a valued teacher, a coach, the parents of a close friend—any adults whose good opinion would matter to the child.

Like an intervention, these adults are all there to express positive regard and sincere concerns, and what they have to say is noncritical, only caring. Their mission is:

- To express concern over specific violence that has happened

- To express all the positive regard in which they hold the child and why
- To express how they each stand ready to be of help to the child in any way they can
- To commit to more communication and contact with the child to keep up with how he is coming along

Confronting Social Reality

If the previous confrontations have failed to persuade, you can put the child on notice that any further acts of violence will cause you to call in social authority by reporting a family disturbance to the police. When the police arrive, describe the incident to the officers, the officers will speak to the child, and the child will have a chance to speak to the police and hear the trouble that additional acts of family violence can bring.

Confronting Outplacement from the Family

If all the previous confrontations fail to persuade the child to cease his acts of family violence, let the child know that you're considering temporary placement outside the family in a highly structured situation to teach him nonviolent ways of living. This could be a treatment facility. This could be a strict residential home. "We want you to be able to live with us, but if you continue to be a danger to the safety of other family members, then you forfeit the right to live among us until you have learned better self-control."

The first step is giving the child this notification. The second step, to show you are serious and to give a picture of what you are talking about, is to visit a treatment or residential facility. And, if the violence continues, the final step is to exit the child from the family for outside help for some period of time. The first step should not be considered unless you are serious and feel temporary outplacement from family can teach the child self-discipline that cannot be taught at home.

DID YOU KNOW?

Sometimes extended family can provide the external placement and learning the violent child needs. For example, a child who is violent in his immediate family may never resort to such destructive acting out while living with grandparents, because he respects them too much and does not want them to experience his violent side.

If you are going to confront the violent child with the possibility of outplacement, it must be presented as a necessary change to preserve safety in the family and not used as a threat, punishment, or banishment. It must be done with love and hope that the child can learn to live by nonviolent choices and soon resume his valued place back in the home.

How to Confront Acts of Self-Violence
Of course, when a willfully violent child turns that violence upon herself by cutting herself or attempting suicide, this calls for a confrontation with a mental health agency or psychiatric unit at a hospital to

get an immediate risk assessment. The child needs to know that you will take any self-destructive behavior so seriously that you will immediately seek outside intervention.

A child's suicide is the act of violence parents most dread. Four common conditions, singly or in combination, in the child's life that can trigger suicidal thoughts can be monitored by parents:

- **Isolation**—the child does not communicate about personal problems or hurt feelings with others
- **Distortion**—the child does not keep a realistic perspective during adversity or stress
- **Despondency**—the child becomes depressed in response to a performance failure or relationship loss
- **Substance abuse**—the child relies on self-medication to escape from unhappiness or pain

Suicidal talk, threats, plans, or attempts must be taken seriously and confronted by the consequence of an external risk assessment. "I didn't really mean I was going to kill myself," protests the child. "I was just kidding to get you upset." Reply the parents, "Suicidal talk is no joking matter. We will check out the seriousness of your intent." Make it known that violence to oneself, just like violence to others, is not an acceptable option.

Chapter 8

How to Handle Discipline

Ten Things You Will Learn in This Chapter

- About the delicate balance of instruction and correction when you discipline your child.

- How to start a conversation with your obstinate child and get to the root of the problem.

- That learning to compromise may save your relationship with your child.

- Why rest is extremely important for a child and how it affects emotional well-being.

- How listing off a set of "parent rules" can help your child understand where you are coming from.

- What an "Earning System" is and why it works.

- What a "Warning System" is and why it works.

- What to do when you feel too exhausted to continue tough parenting tactics.

- Four ways to keep your disciplining effective and not inflammatory.

- About the major delivery systems for discipline— guidance, supervision, structure, and working the exchange points.

What's Your Goal?

Discipline is the combination of parental instruction and parental correction through which a child is taught to live according to family values and to act within family rules. Since no two families subscribe to exactly the same values and rules, every child learns a unique pattern of behavior and carries a unique code of personal conduct into adulthood. Parents, through the examples they model (how to be and how not to be) and by the discipline they provide, are responsible for shaping the beliefs and conduct of their child. They also provide discipline when the child is unable to properly discipline himself.

A BETTER PARENTING PRACTICE

With a willful child, the best parents can do is work for compromise. They must accept that they will not get their way all the time, only some of the time, to some degree. This is a realistic expectation: some has to be enough. The same expectation holds for the willful child. Only some of the time, to some degree, will she get her way.

The ultimate goal of parental discipline is to work parents out of their job. Parental discipline aims to teach the child sufficient self-discipline to successfully manage a responsible self-supporting and self-governing independence. To keep discipline effective, it needs to be 90 percent instructional and positive and no more than 10 percent corrective and negative. When this ratio becomes reversed, as so easily happens with a willful child, particularly with a willful adolescent, the boy's or girl's behavior becomes worse, not better. As the relationship with parents loses positive value for the child, the child's willingness to comply with what parents want is also lost. "Why should I want to do what my parents want when all they ever do is complain, criticize, and punish me?"

Relying exclusively on corrective measures "to change" your willful child only encourages more resistance in return. "And we'll keep punishing you until your attitude improves!" But the outcome of their efforts is a more sullen, not a more cheerful, child. The most powerful incentive for desirable behavior parents can provide is ongoing affirmation for who and how the child is.

Strong-willed children often test and contest parental rules and directions because they are so self-determined and independently inclined. The job of parents is not to get 100 percent compliance. That is not a realistic expectation. The parents' job is to keep asserting those family rules and values, and to keep modeling constructive habits of behavior, to encourage the child to choose to follow a healthy path in life. When parents get discouraged by the child's resistance and give up providing disciplinary leadership, they deprive the child of the opportunity for healthy choice. Parents who relinquish this leadership, by default give their child other, less caring and reliable influences (like peers) to follow.

Learning to Respect Choice

Strong-willed children want to be self-directed. What willfulness wants most of all is some measure of personal choice. So, when your child is acting most obstinate or insistent, it is always worth questioning her: "Tell me why, help me understand why making this decision is so important to you." Sometimes your empathy with the child's intense desire for self-determination can avert automatic acting out by opening up a discussion that allows you to influence the choice being made.

DID YOU KNOW?

A rested child is more inclined to cooperate than an exhausted child is. A calm child is more inclined to listen than one who is emotionally upset. Therefore, it is in the interests of effective discipline to keep your willful child adequately rested and to encourage calmness by acting calm yourself.

Instead of the parent's immediately censoring a dress decision, the mother asks why the child is making that decision. So the child explains, "I'm going to tear my jeans at the knee because that's the different look I want to wear to school. I don't want to be like everyone else." "Thank you for helping me understand," replies the parent. "Now I understand that you are not wanting to trash your new jeans. You want to dress in your own individual way. How about this? Suppose I help you bleach the knees so they look worn, but are untorn? Would you be willing to try that?" And so understanding mother and willful child reach a working compromise—more than the mother wanted but less than the child desired.

Separation of Powers

Your willful child needs to know that the only choices you, as parent, are concerned with controlling are your own. When the child says "You can't make me!" or "You can't stop me!" you need to immediately agree. "That's right. Your choices are always up to you, just as my choices are always up to me."

Then you need to repeat one more time the "parent rules"—the rules you are duty bound to follow in order to be a responsible parent to your child. You can preface the rules by saying something like this: "Being a responsible parent isn't always easy, popular, or fun, because I sometimes have to make decisions you don't agree with or like. Because these decisions will sometimes be opposed to what you want, you may think I am not on your side. But that is not true. When I take a stand against what you want, it is for what I believe are your best interests." Then state the parent rules: "I am supposed to:

- Set limits and requirements to keep you safe
- Tell you information and teach you skills you need to know
- Keep after you to get tasks done and to build healthy habits
- Model values and set positive examples for you to follow
- Determine which freedoms are okay now and which must wait

- Give you more work and responsibility as you grow
- Provide for your care until you are able to support yourself
- Listen when we disagree and be willing to have the final say
- Commit to the fact that, no matter how we disagree, you will always have my love."

Choice-for-Choice Contracting

"Why should I?" asks the willful child, objecting to a request or a demand. Sometimes, in response, a parental explanation can persuade: "Because I'm busy doing the cooking and I need your help."

At other times, however, you need to appeal to the child's self-interest by connecting his personal choice with your parental response if he does not comply as asked. While respecting the willful child's power of choice, you must also teach the child to respect your power of choice. Parents can explain choice-for-choice contracting like this:

- "Your choices are entirely up to you."
- "My choices are entirely up to me."
- "If you agree to do what I ask, this is what I will choose to do."
- "If you refuse to do what I ask, this is what I will choose to do."
- "Which response I give depends a lot on choices of your own."

To be effective, choice-for-choice contracting should not be done in anger or as a threat. State it matter-of-factly, as you would when describing how some household mechanism works. You are giving information and notification. "It's pretty simple, really. If you choose this, then I choose that." After your child makes her choice (to do her chores, to give you help, to abide by your rule), follow through as stated. "Because you chose to help me, I choose to do what you asked." You empower the child by respecting her choice and giving her influence over your chosen behavior in response.

DID YOU KNOW?

Come early adolescence (ages nine to thirteen), earning and warning systems become less effective, as the more rebellious boy or girl now sees these tactics as power plays by parents and refuses to go along. "When you tell me what you'll give me if I do what you want, that's not a reward, that's a threat! If I don't do what you want, then I don't get what you promised! No way!"

Earning Systems and Warning Systems

With preadolescent children, up to about age eight or nine, two time-honored kinds of choice-for-choice contracting are earning systems and warning systems. Both systems give children a chance to think ahead and weigh personal choice in light of consequences that can follow—the kind of choice parents will make in response.

Earning systems attach credits to cooperative choices; warning systems attach penalties to noncooperative choices. Using an earning system, the parent can promise, "If you feed the dog every day this week, come the weekend you will have earned my taking you and a friend out for the lunch of your choice." Using a warning system, the parent can promise, "If by the count of three you have not ended your game and started setting the table for supper, you will get no dessert." In each case, the child has the choice to make the system work in his favor or not—choice for choice.

Make Sure You're Consistent!

What are the three most important principles in effectively disciplining a strong-willed child? Consistency, consistency, and consistency.

- Consistently clarify what you want and do not want to have happen. "You will come home at the time we agreed and you will not be late."
- Consistently commit to back up what you want. "If you are late, I will come and get you, and for a while you will have less freedom to go out than you had before."
- Consistently continue to restate and back up what you want. "As before, when you go over to a friend's, I want to set a time for your return that you agree to honor."

Parental consistency does not guarantee 100 percent compliance from a strong-willed child, but it does help maximize the influence you have. It is in the nature of a willful child to test rules, demands, and limits, to see if they are firm or flexible, to see if you are just making noise or are actually taking stands. It is as if the willful child is thinking, "The only way to know if my parents mean business about what I can and cannot do is to disobey and see what happens. If they don't back off or back down, then I know they're serious."

When it comes to respecting parental demands and limits, willful children are often not one-trial learners. They will test and contest what they are told to see if what is said is real, if parents really mean what they say. Say it and show that you mean it often and consistently enough, and you stand a good chance of turning your willful child into a believer.

Making Rules Stick

It is tiring to be consistent, to repeatedly state and stick to what you say when you're tired and feel like slacking off. But being inconsistent with a willful child is even more exhausting because of the double message you send: "Sometimes we mean what we say and sometimes we don't." Just as a willful child comes to respect the firmness of "always," he or she can find it hard to resist exploiting the weakness of "sometimes."

Identifying Compliance

When tired parents become discouraged into believing that they have lost all influence with their willful child, it can be helpful to locate a baseline of compliance. To do so, parents need to answer a simple but significant question: "Where does our willful child regularly and without protest do what we ask?"

At first, out of frustration, parents may declare, "Nowhere!" But on sober reflection, they will be able to find some area of discipline where the child always seems to give compliance. Because this area feels like the exception to the rule of argument and resistance, the parents have paid it scant attention. What a mistake! They ignore where their discipline is working and why.

The parents may grudgingly admit, "He never gives us trouble at bedtime. He gets right in, on time, with no delay or complaint." Why is that? "Because," they explain, "he knows that by the end of the day we're in no mood to put up with any nonsense and we want some adult time by ourselves." And how does he know? "From experience," they say. "One thing we've never given an inch on is his bedtime. We've made our expectations clear from the beginning. He takes it for granted because that's how we've always been."

And once they realize that, they can recognize that as the baseline model for getting compliance. That's the one area of discipline they've consistently shown to be non-negotiable and therefore not worth challenging. So now they must apply this to other areas of his behavior to get compliance.

Don't Make the Situation Worse!

With a willful child, the first guideline for parents is to not inflame the situation by unwittingly inciting or increasing the child's predisposition to resist. To this end, there are four principles of noninflammatory discipline that parents should consistently follow.

Keep Discipline Nonemotional

The more calm, reasoned, and matter-of-fact parents act, the more they encourage that quality of response. "As we agreed the last time, if you take and break your brother's toy again, you will have to use what money you've saved to buy him another." Mix discipline with emotional intensity and a willful child will become emotional in response.

➧ DID YOU KNOW?

There's a learning curve for everything, including discipline. Parents who learn to teach discipline the fastest, and children who learn to accept discipline the fastest, both depend on one factor more than on any other: consistency of parental instruction and correction.

Keep Discipline Nonevaluative

The less critical and judgmental parents act when giving a correction, the less likely the willful child will become defensive in return. Practice this mantra of correction until it becomes second nature: "We disagree with the choice you have made; this is why, and this is what we need to have happen in consequence." Correction is criticism enough.

Keep Discipline Nonargumentative

The more you debate whether a behavior was wrong or whether your disciplinary response to that misbehavior is right, the more argument you encourage. The more invested in changing your mind the willful child becomes, the more he believes resolution is a matter of competition, the angrier he feels when he discovers it is not. Explain, but don't debate. Be willing to discuss to understand. Don't be willing to argue to win.

Keep Discipline Noncoercive

The more you try to emotionally or physically force your way, the more you threaten to take away or overwhelm the willful child's decision-making power, the more determined to fight to preserve that power the child becomes. Instead, simply explain the choice you need the child to make, and then explain what will be your responses to compliance or noncompliance. Force makes things worse, not better.

Guidance, Supervision, and Structure

Of the four major delivery systems for discipline—guidance, supervision, structure, and working the exchange points—guidance is the most influential because it offers the most instructional power. The purpose of guidance is to guide the child with the best information and understanding you can provide. This is accomplished by giving constant feedback about which choices the child is making that are working well and which choices are not. Guidance is how parents talk and talk and talk to the child to support good decisions, to discourage bad ones, to advise, to inform, to editorialize, and to educate about life. Children who are blessed with a parent who is not afraid to speak up always know where that parent stands, always have an adult reference to guide them, always can count on an honest response to how they are conducting their life.

DID YOU KNOW?

Communication is the most powerful source of parental influence in general, and it's the most powerful response to an infraction that parents have to give. Your constant guidance is not designed to control the child's choice (which you cannot do) but to continually inform the child's choice about what good lessons can be learned from bad experiences and what is wise.

Why Children Resist Guidance

With a strong-willed child, parental guidance can be resisted and resented on the principle of independence. "You don't have to tell me! I know all about it! I don't have to be told! I don't need your opinion! I can figure it out!" Self-determined to be left to his or her own devices, the willful child doesn't want the parent butting in. But "butting in" with a mature perspective is a parent's job. Otherwise, the child will be left at the mercy of personal ignorance and the ignorance of peers.

"But," protests the parent, "what's the point of giving guidance if my child doesn't want to hear what I say, doesn't understand the importance of what I say, doesn't agree with what I say, and doesn't do what I say? Why waste the words?"

It is never a waste to give guidance to your child, because children always listen to their parents (although parents don't always listen to their children). Whether the child wants to hear what you have to say, understands the importance of what you say, agrees with what you say, or actually does what you say has no bearing on the value of the guidance you give. The value of parental guidance is the mature, caring, adult frame of reference for making decisions and the perspective for sorting out what is happening in the child's world. The first purpose of guidance is for parents to define for the child what they believe and where they stand.

How to give guidance to a willful child is the issue. You don't want to give guidance in any way that is likely to make the child defensive. So refrain from criticism, argument, worry, anger, threats, and emotional upset in general. These will not keep the child from hearing what you have to say, but they will reduce the likelihood of crediting and using what you have to say.

Effective guidance is not in the business of forcing your opinion or changing the child's mind. Thus, instead of challenging the child's belief, formed by trusted middle school peer informants, that inhalants can't do any harm, simply offer an alternative perspective: "I understand what you've been told. Here is another way to think about huffing inhalants. Good scientific research has shown that those chemicals can permanently damage the brain. Just so you know."

Creating Talking Points

Because the willful child is so insistent on self-determination, he or she is apt to be defensive when called out for making a mistake or having a problem, treating this parental response as a criticism for not taking care of business effectively. "I know, I know! Just get the punishment over with. I don't want to talk about it!" The willful child just wants to be done with the correction, omit the discussion, and go on about his business.

A BETTER PARENTING PRACTICE

In general, don't assign more chores than you have energy to supervise. If you commit to more demands than you can supervise, you risk encouraging your willful child to exploit the inconsistency of your attention because it appears that you "didn't really mean it."

But correction should never be the primary consequence when a willful child gets into difficulty or commits an infraction. The primary consequence needs to be communication and instruction, extracting guidance from an unhappy situation by turning what happened into a talking point so the child can learn from hard experience. "I will let you know later about what restitution you need to make for what you did. First off, however, you and I will discuss how you got into that situation, what led you to make that decision, and how you can avoid getting into that kind of trouble again.

Although I wish this hadn't happened, since it did, I want you to be able to learn all you can from the experience so you'll be better informed and better advised from now on."

Education before evaluation, communication before consequence, instruction before correction: these are the rules of guidance when your child runs into difficulty or misbehaves.

Supervision

The second major delivery system for discipline is supervision—the willingness of parents to relentlessly keep after the willful child to do what she has been asked or has agreed to do.

Supervision is nagging. It is honorable, onerous work, part of the drudgework of parenting. If there are two parents in the home, it needs to be shared, otherwise inequity in parental supervision can become divisive of the marriage. The nagging parent is resented for her thankless efforts by the child and feels resentful toward the other parent who is better liked because of how he lets supervision go.

When parents supervise, they demonstrate with their repeating and reminding that they mean business about what they asked or to what the child agreed. "And I'll keep after you and after you and after you until your chores get done."

When supervising a willful child, you must beware of unwittingly encouraging the child's resistance by becoming impatient, frustrated, and emotionally upset. Effective supervision requires emotionally sober insistence. Keep emotions out of it. When parents get frustrated and angry in their pursuit, the child learns that delay has the power to get them emotionally worked up. Therefore, when in the process of supervision you feel yourself emotionally heating up, pass supervision on to the other parent, or take a break, cool down, and then take up the pursuit again. Remember, part of being a willful child is a dislike of being directed, interfered with, or interrupted. When it comes to supervision, effective parents never give up.

Structure

The third major delivery system for discipline is structure—the willingness of parents to specify major rules of social conduct that the child is expected to obey. These are the limitations and obligations that you intend to hold your child responsible for observing. For example, "Within the family there is no hurtful name calling, no hitting, and no taking of other people's belongings allowed; and you will keep your promises, tell us the truth, and communicate in a respectful way." These prohibitions and obligations communicate basic parental values and provide a basic structural framework within which "good" habits of behavior can be learned.

The structure of rules that parents provide is only as strong as the parents' determination to enforce these rules with consequences when children violate them. When it comes to providing structure, parents have three responsibilities: to explain the rules, to enforce the rules, and to express appreciation for following the rules. Effective parents consistently articulate rules, enforce established rules, and reward compliance with rules.

Willful children, because they are inclined to play by their own rules, often question parental rules. You must expect these questions, answer as honestly as you can ("Because we want to keep you safe," "Because this is a value we believe in"), and then stand by your rule when the child pronounces your explanation not good enough.

Consequences for Violations of Rules

When a child breaks a rule, you apply consequences to catch the child's attention, cause him to rethink what happened, and hopefully discourage him from repeating that choice again. The goal of punishment is to teach a lesson that convinces the child not to repeat the infraction. Three powerful consequences are natural consequences, a good talking-to, and reparation, which can help your child make up for what he did.

Natural consequences are often sufficient to teach a corrective lesson without parents having to add any additional consequences of their own. Going against the rules, the child plays with fire and gets burned. Lesson learned.

A good talking-to is often the most disliked consequence of all. "And you're going to sit here and listen for as long as it takes me to say everything I want to say about what I feel and think about what you've done." After ten minutes, the chastened child asks, "Are you done?" Replies the steadfast parent, "Honey, I'm not even warmed up yet!" Children hate a "lecture" most of all.

Reparation is giving the rule breaker some extra work to do she would not normally have to do before she gets to do anything else she wants. Reparation is much more influential than deprivation ("grounding" in its various forms) because the child has to do something active to work off the offense. Some parents keep a list of jobs in need of doing around the home posted on the refrigerator door—jobs that can be accomplished through reparation work should major violations occur. To work as reparations, these jobs must go be in addition to the regular chores that your child already does.

A BETTER PARENTING PRACTICE

If you feel you must use deprivation, never, ever punish a willful adolescent by taking away a pillar of self-esteem—an interest or activity or relationship in which the child invests and gains self-affirmation in return. The more you cause the adolescent to feel bad about himself, worsening his self-esteem, the less he will want to cooperate with you. Pillars of self-esteem are sacred and should never be subject to deprivation. Take away something else.

Object Lessons

Because the willful child is so self-determined, it sometimes takes a hard lesson to teach the child the error of her ways. Object lessons can sometimes provide this education in powerfully convincing ways. With an object lesson, you set up a situation in which the child learns from experience what words alone are unable to teach.

Imagine a child who insists he won't do anything his parents ask unless they pay him. "Why should I work for you for free?" So the parent, who understands that arguing the issue of free family service with such a willful child is doomed to failure, agrees to this, saying, "This has to go both ways. I'll pay you a dollar for doing everything I ask, and you pay me a dollar for everything I do for you. Okay?" And the child happily agrees, collecting several dollars that night for clearing the supper table, for changing the cat's litter box, and for picking up his clothes that had been thrown on the floor. What a great system!

Next morning, the child asks for a clean shirt to wear to school. "That will be a dollar," says the parent. Then the child wants some shampoo to wash his hair. "That will be a dollar," says the parent. Then the child comes in for breakfast. "That will be a dollar," says the parent. Then the child, now out of money, wants lunch for school. "That will be a dollar," says the parent. "But I haven't got a dollar," complains the child. "I paid them all back!" "Then," explains the parent sympathetically, "I guess you'll have to go to school without lunch." "But this isn't fair!" objects the child, now that the system of paid service is working against and not for him. "Well," suggests the parent, "why don't you think about the system of freely doing for each other we had before, and we can talk about going back to that when you get home from school, at the free supper I'm going to fix for you tonight."

Exchange Points

The fourth major delivery system for discipline is working the exchange points—exploiting the child's dependency on parents to encourage cooperation with parents by withholding daily services, resources, or permissions until the child does something they requested first. This is neither a threat nor a punishment. If anything, it is a kind of object lesson that teaches the child how giving is required for getting.

"I'd be happy to drive you over to your friend's house, but before I do, please take out the trash as I asked." To which the impatient child responds, "I promise I will when I get back!" No. Promises are false currency. They have repeatedly been used to get the parent to make a bad bargain—to do for the child only to have the child renege on the agreement later on. So the parent holds firm. "I'm happy to drive you, but the trash must be taken out first."

If your willful child is highly resistant to doing chores, just wait for the next exchange point and condition your cooperation on getting household work you want accomplished first. When it comes to working the exchange points, effective parents make sure they get before they give.

Chapter 9

How to Handle Conflict

Ten Things You Will Learn in This Chapter

- About the nature of conflict and when it is most likely to arise.

- The answer to your question: "How can we stop fighting all the time?"

- How to choose when to cooperate in conflict and when to avoid it.

- What you can learn from your verbal conflicts.

- How to learn from conflict and become closer in it's aftermath.

- Buzz words and helpful sayings to end an ineffective conflict.

- Why teaching "sticks and stones may break my bones but words will never hurt me" is wrong!

- The certain blame statements that a parent should never say.

- What questions to ask to get a conflict resolved and learn from it.

- When to avoid conflict and when you NEED to address it.

The Nature of Conflict

If you have a child who is by nature willful, or if you have a child who is growing through a willful phase like adolescence, it is realistic to expect more conflict with that self-determined boy or girl. Because opposition can be frustrating, family conflict is often an emotionally arousing experience. Therefore, the number one priority for all parties involved is not resolving the issue at difference, but rather managing emotional arousal so it does not cause anyone to do or say anything that anyone has later cause to regret.

Conflict is the process through which people clarify, confront, and resolve inevitable human differences between them. The more human diversity there is in families (and stepfamilies have even more than the biological kind), the more occasions for conflict there is likely to be. Conflicts between parents, parents and child, and child and child are built into family life when any of four categories of common questions are raised.

- Who gets to do what? Who gets to get what? What is a fair share?
- Control creates conflict. Who is in charge? Who makes the rules? Whose is the right way?
- Competition creates conflict. Who wins? Who gets the most? Who goes first?
- Conformity creates conflict. Who sets the norm? Who has to fit in? Who gets to act different?

Conflict Takes Cooperation

"Our child is so stubborn, she fights with us about everything. It's just exhausting. How can we stop her from fighting with us all the time?" The answer is simple: stop fighting back. It takes two to make a conflict. The opposition must be mutual. One resistance pushing against another resistance is the formula for conflict. Remember the bumper sticker slogan, "Suppose they gave a war and nobody came?" Or only one side came? There would be no battle. Suppose the willful child wants an argument, but neither parent is so inclined. To stop arguments, simply refuse to argue back.

Contrary to common sense, conflict is not about disagreement. Conflict is a matter of agreement—two parties agreeing to disagree over some common issue at difference between them. Should homework be done immediately? Your twelve-year-old thinks instant messaging to friends matters more. You take a stand for homework first. She argues. You insist. She grudgingly consents. A conflict arose because you both agreed to disagree about homework. In this case, resolution was in your favor. But just to make sure you check her quickly accomplished work for careless errors and omissions.

Conflict is always a matter of agreement—parents agreeing to contest a difference that their willful child agrees to contest with them. Parents don't have to cooperate in any more conflict than they want to. They always have a choice. Since parents cannot afford the energy to fight over every difference that arises, they must pick their battles wisely.

Conflict Is Informative

Many parents do not appreciate the educational value of conflict with their willful child. Verbal conflict is an act of communication. The child is speaking up and sharing information about what she wants, what she values, how she thinks, and how she sees the world. Conflict is just two different ways of looking at the same issue. It provides a window into the other person's point of view.

DID YOU KNOW?

Conflict usually stresses parents more than it stresses the child. Afterward, parents want to collapse and rest, whereas their child isn't even breathing hard. Therefore, don't cooperate in more conflict than you have purpose to justify and energy to afford.

For example, consider the battle over posters on the bedroom wall. "We are not having you decorate your room with posters of any rock group called Nasty Manners!" Argues the child, "I want those band posters in my room because the music matters to me. It's all about unfairness and anger and getting your emotions out. Don't you understand? When I look at the pictures and listen to the music, it helps calm my feelings down!"

Parents who consider conflict with their willful child only a matter of winning or losing miss out on using conflict as a great talking point, a chance to understand their child more deeply than before, and as a chance to become better known themselves. Conflict creates an opportunity for dialogue.

DID YOU KNOW?

Parental guidance is in the business of informing the child's understanding, not controlling the child's choice. In caring relationships, the primary goal of conflict is not supremacy, but intimacy. There are two avenues for intimacy. First, by sharing similarities, people create commonality. And second, by being willing to disagree, people create understanding about natural differences between them. People who never fight are people with half an intimacy—they either avoid or ignore important diversity in their relationships.

When parent and willful child declare, after a conflict, that they understand each other better than they did before, then conflict has fulfilled its function. A deeper intimacy has been established. "I can see why you got so upset at my fooling around with alcohol," the child says. "I never knew before about all the problems it caused in your family growing up."

Conflict Is Formative

Conflict is not something you have with your willful child. It is something you *do* with your willful child. Conflict is a performance act. Every time you do conflict with your child, by experience, example, and instruction, you teach your child how to conduct conflict. So, when you model sticking to specifics, staying on the subject, avoiding extreme statements, keeping in the present, speaking for yourself, taking responsibility for your position, hearing the other person out, and being empathetic and nonjudgmental, you give your child productive behaviors to follow. In addition, when he interrupts or calls names ("You're being really stupid!"), you instructionally intervene. "I'm willing to continue discussing our disagreement, but I don't interrupt you or call you demeaning names, and I don't want you doing that to me."

A BETTER PARENTING PRACTICE

When it comes to safety violations in family conflict, any injury that occurs should be by accident, not intentional. When one family member violates the rule of safety with another, all members of the family are affected—"It really scared me when Daddy blew up at you!" "Losing control" in conflict is never really loss of control. It's one person resorting to extreme measures to try and get his or her way.

Another formative part of conflict has to do with the equation that now equals later. How your child learns to do conflict with you now is how he or she will conduct conflict with other people later on. When you engage in conflict with your child, you are training him in how conflict can be productively and safely conducted. Thus, you explain to your willful child, who, frustrated by your opposition, has just behaved in a physically threatening manner, how this behavior can not only hurt you now, but also can hurt him later on.

"When I tell you that acting like you are going to hit me is unacceptable because it is unsafe, I am telling you this not just for my own good, but for yours. If I let you get away with this behavior now, there is the possibility that further down the road of life, when in conflict, you will repeat this behavior with someone you really care about. And that person, finding you unsafe to disagree with, may choose to end the relationship, and you will end up hurting yourself, perhaps losing a friend or someone you love."

If you commit verbal, emotional, or physical injury in family conflict, the trustful nature of that relationship can be seriously damaged or lost. This is why the first rule in family conflict is safety. "Sticks and stones can break my bones but words can never hurt me" is simply not true. In family conflict, words do most of the damage. Like other animals, people fight with their mouths. So watch what you say. "I'm sorry" cannot undo the damage done. The only acceptable amends is never committing such injury again.

Who's Responsible?

Conflict is a mutually agreed upon opposition over an issue at difference between two or more parties. Parents may disagree over how to correct their child for breaking a family rule. Parent and child may disagree over the necessity of the child's doing a chore. Children may disagree over whose turn it is to play with a toy. In these cases, each party is responsible for contributing to the active opposition between them.

The problem is, responsibility can be hard to take. Parents and child often like to blame the other person for the conflict. "We're only arguing because you're wrong," says one parent to the other. "If you'd just do what you're told, we wouldn't have to fight about it," says the parent to the child. "He started it!" protests one child about the other. In each case, the speaker is disavowing responsibility for the conflict and assigning it to the other party.

DID YOU KNOW?

Some parental blame statements cut children to the core. "How could you do this to us?" "You really let us down!" "You've disappointed us!" "You should be ashamed!" "You've ruined your life!" "You're nothing but a problem!" Blame can do a lot of harm.

Placing Blame

In the short run, blame can make people feel better by excusing them of any complicity in their own trouble or unhappiness. In the long run, however, it only attacks the blamed and victimizes the blamer. If the trouble or unhappiness is entirely the other person's fault, then the other person is both accused and empowered, and the blamer is helpless to stop or influence what is going on.

"Our child keeps the family in a constant state of upset!" With this statement of blame, parents cast off power of responsibility to change an unhappy situation. To improve the situation at home, they have to reclaim their share of responsibility. "Just because our child is constantly acting out doesn't mean we always have to get upset in response. In fact, our response may be only encouraging his acting out." Come a willful child's adolescence, it is common for parents and teenager to blame each other with the same complaints. The other party:

- "Never listens to what I say"
- "Never appreciates all I do"
- "Never does what I want"

Blame and complaints, as natural as they are, do not resolve conflicts; they only intensify them. The blamed party often blames the blamer back, and soon the conflict over who is going to do or get what, or over who is right and who is wrong, has escalated into accusations over who is the sorrier human being.

DID YOU KNOW?

Learning to fight well is the work of a lifetime. By victimizing the blamer and offending and empowering the blamed, blame only makes conflicts worse, never better. By accepting personal responsibility for one's share in conflict, each person is best able to resolve it.

Replacing Blame with Responsibility

Anytime you find yourself blaming, or about to blame, your willful child for a conflict, remember that when you do you only empower her (now she is in more control) and reduce your influence (now there is less you can do). Instead, ask yourself three responsibility questions:

- What degree of cooperative responsibility are you willing to accept for your share in the conflict? "As soon as she gets home from school, I tell my child to begin her chores and we immediately get into an argument."
- What are you willing to do differently to change the interaction? "I might ask her how her day was and suggest she take a break to relax before helping me around the home."
- What are you willing to give in order to get what you want? "I might give her more choice over when the chores get done, later than I ideally would like but delayed enough to encourage her cooperation."

Conflict Resolution

Resolution of conflict is how you and your child come to agreement over what to do about the difference on which you both have agreed to disagree. Who is responsible? Which is the right way? What needs to happen? When will it be done? Why is that necessary? How much should be allowed?

Every conflict can be stated as a question, and every resolution is an attempt to answer that question in a way both parties can accept. This doesn't mean that both parties necessarily like the resolution, only that both agree to accept it. If the resolution is a compromise, for example, this means that, on a personal level, resolution is going to be a losing proposition. Each party agrees to take less than 100 percent of what each ideally wants to settle the divisive issue between them. So the willful thirteen-year-old pushes to stay out longer than parents really want, but agrees to come home earlier than other friends who have been allowed a later curfew. On a relationship level, compromises are a winning proposition because conflict over a difference has been successfully resolved, and the relationship has been strengthened by reaching a settlement both agree to honor.

DOES THIS SOUND LIKE YOUR CHILD?

Do not get into proprietary conflicts with your willful child, trying to change what only the child can control. "I'll go potty when I want!" "You can't make me eat!" "Going to sleep is up to me!" Simply explain why you believe it is in his or her best interests to do what you agree only the child can ultimately decide to do, and encourage the child to try.

Strategies for Resolving Conflict

Left to her own self-preoccupation, the willful child often thinks that there are only three options for resolving conflict: "My way" (I win), "Your way" (I lose), or "No way" (we can't resolve the difference). Left to their own frustration, parents can think the same. Both need to subscribe to a fourth option: "Our way" (an agreement we can both accept can be reached).

There are many ways for resolving conflict, and with a willful child, with whom conflict is a frequent occurrence, parents need a variety of resolution strategies at their disposal. The more choices they have, the more freedom of flexibility they will feel. Consider just a few of the more common choices.

Change

You and your child are in conflict over picking up her backpack where she has dumped it in the hall when she and a friend came home from school. After ignoring your demand, she says she'll do it later. "Do it now!" you command. And when she refuses, you take her into the other room to discuss the problem. "If you'd ask instead of tell, I might," she says. "I won't be ordered around in front of friends." So you decide to make a change in your approach. Ten minutes later, you interrupt the two friends with a request for your daughter: "I'd really appreciate it if you'd take your backpack to your room." "Sure," she agrees. She saves face, and you get cooperation.

Concession

You have a rule that, until your child is in the fourth grade, he can't sleep over at a friend's house. But in the third grade, his best friend is having a slumber party on his birthday and he has been invited and wants to go. "I feel silly missing the party since all of my friends will be there!" Weighing your concerns for safety with his needs for social belonging, you decide to make a concession, especially since he will be well supervised by his best friend's parents at the party. "I think this issue is more important for you than it is for me, so I agree to let you have what you want, so long as you remain mindful of the rules of safety you've been taught. Another time when we have a disagreement, when the issue is more important to me, I'd like you to go along with me."

Chance

Yet again, your two children are fighting over who gets to go first. Rather than get into an endless discussion to determine what is fair, you offer to resolve the issue by chance: "I'll flip a coin, and the winner gets to go first." And both children agree to abide by that decision.

Compromise

Your child wants your help on a school project but doesn't want to start working on it until the night before, using last-minute deadline pressure as a motivator for overcoming resistance to completing what she doesn't want to do. You don't want to give last-minute help because that feels too stressful. So you reach a compromise. If she agrees to begin work two nights before it's due, you will agree to give help under somewhat less stressful conditions. You each sacrificed some self-interest to get what you could both live with.

Creative Alternative

You've offered to take the kids out to eat, but they immediately disagree on what restaurant they want, and the outing has become obstructed by the conflict

between them. It seems like an either/or situation, either
one child's choice or the other's, until you reframe the
choice in a larger way. "Why we are really going out is
not just to eat, but to have fun together. So rather than
get bogged down in where to eat, let's think about some
other activity that would be fun for us all." So you end
up going bowling instead. You opened up a choice that
was outside the limited alternatives posed by the original opposition between them.

A BETTER PARENTING PRACTICE

When you are about to engage in conflict with your
child, instead of going for control, try expressing
concern. Rather than make a critical response—
"What's the matter with you?"—try making an
empathetic response instead: "Are you feeling
okay?" The child may feel less defensive and more
receptive to discussion.

Avoid Emotional Extortion

A willful child, or a willful parent, bent on winning a
conflict can resort to manipulation, which works in the
short run but builds ill feeling into the relationship over
time. Either party can choose to use emotional extortion to get his way.

What is emotional extortion? Rather than declare
what he wants and discuss and negotiate a resolution,
the willful child or willful parent can try to force agreement by using the strong expression of emotion to get
the other person to relent.

- He can use the expression of love to cajole and flatter.
- He can use the expression of anger (loudly or silently) to communicate rejection.
- He can use the expression of suffering to elicit guilt.
- He can use the expression of helplessness to play on pity.
- He can use the expression of apathy to signify abandonment of caring.
- He can combine anger and suffering into a tantrum to intimidate.
- He can use the expression of violence to threaten physical injury.

When parent or child gives in to any of these emotional ploys, he ends up feeling manipulated and resentful and distrustful on that account. And the relationship suffers. So don't use emotional extortion yourself, and if your willful child ever uses it on you, simply respond by saying, "Expressing strong feeling is not going to get me to change my mind or cause me to agree. Tell me what it is you want or do not want to have happen, and we can talk it out." Take the child out of an emotionally manipulative mode and into a rationally declarative one.

Conflict Avoidance

Because conflict takes so much energy, parents cannot afford to become embroiled in every opportunity for conflict that a willful child offers. "It's bedtime," declares the parent. "No, it's not," disagrees the child. "It's too early and I'm not tired yet." "Your bedtime," explains the parent, "isn't just about your need for rest. It's about my need for rest, too. Right now I am tired enough for you to go to bed and too tired to discuss the point. So, good night." And the child, being given no further opening for argument, wearily gives up the fight for the night, but not for tomorrow.

A BETTER PARENTING PRACTICE

If you lack adequate conflict-avoidance skills, you risk getting entrapped in more conflict than you have energy for. To avoid excessive conflict: let angry provocations go, refuse to further justify demands you have already explained, and back up your stands with firm insistence, refusing to back down.

It's not just that willful children have more energy for conflict than their parents do; willful children are energized by conflict in ways their parents typically are not. For willful children, conflict is challenging and stimulating. It provides an opportunity to assert self-interest that many willful children value. "Parents are good to practice my arguing on. And there's always a chance that I can change their mind."

So when it comes to conflict, the keys for parents of a willful child are to be selective, to not engage in any more conflict than they have energy and purpose to confront, and to avoid those invitations (or provocations) into conflict that are not worth their while.

When to Avoid Conflict

Sometimes a willful child, feeling up for a fight, will challenge parents by throwing out an extreme statement about what he is going or not going to do: "I'm going to run away, and you can't stop me!" "I'm never going back to that school, and you can't make me!" Willful challenges are either statements of frustration or invitations to conflict.

DID YOU KNOW?

There are two conditions under which parents should not avoid conflict with their willful child. First, if parents are doing so out of intimidation, because then they will end up giving their child extortionate power over their fear. And second, if by doing so parents run the risk of escalation—the longer they delay confronting an issue, the more volatile it gets.

For parents, such extreme statements can be scary. Taking them literally and becoming frightened, they can be seduced into taking a stand over a threat ("Oh, no you're not!") or making extreme statements in return ("If you refuse, I'll ship you off to military school!"). And the willful child gets the angry outlet or argument he was after.

So what should parents do when a willful challenge comes their way? Leave the challenge on the table. Don't argue with it. Don't credit it with truth. After all, if the child were really going to run away or refuse to return to school, he wouldn't waste time putting you on notice.

He'd be doing it. He just wants to create a forum for frustration or a conflict around this issue.

So, say something like this: "Well, it seems to me that decision would cause you more problems than benefits, but your choices are certainly up to you. Of course, if there are feelings behind this decision you would like to discuss, I'd be happy to hear what you have to say." Let the child know you don't think the proposal is a good idea, but you take your opposition off the table. Place responsibility for carrying through with the decision firmly on the child. You make no emotional reaction to the proposal. And you offer to listen if there are feelings attached to this proposal that the child wants to share.

When Not to Avoid Conflict

Some parents may say, "I would rather put up with what I don't like than fight about it with my child." But there are definite dangers to avoiding conflict.

- If you tiptoe around sensitive issues that get your child angry, you increase your fear of the child's anger.
- If you let some of your child's unacceptable behavior go, you will increasingly choose to live on your child's unacceptable terms.
- If you keep quiet about your child's offensive behavior, you will store up resentment toward the child.
- If you avoid talking out differences, you will tend to imagine and distort what is really going on with the child.

- If you stuff your own declaration of anger, you risk building it up for a later blowup over something not related to the first offense.
- If you don't dare talk about a divisive issue, you will lose an opportunity for dialogue and intimacy that conflict has to offer.
- If you keep avoiding conflict, you will develop a habit of avoidance that can be hard to break.
- If you keep avoiding conflict, you will weaken your capacity to resolve differences in a satisfactory way.

Blustering Tactics

Parents of a willful adolescent need to expect several common blustering tactics designed to discourage parents from raising issues the teenager doesn't want to discuss. To escape discussion, the teenager tries to bully the parent into avoidance.

- **Protective belligerence:** "Don't mess with me, I'm in a bad mood!"
- **Protective busyness:** "Not now; can't you see I'm doing something important!"
- **Protective unavailability:** "I've got to leave; we can talk about it later!"

So when is a good time to have a sensitive talk with your willful teenager? There isn't one. You are often going to be given a hard time dealing with something the teenager doesn't want to discuss. So don't let adolescent blustering tactics scare you off. Brave your adolescent's disapproval and choose any old bad time to have your say.

Sibling Conflict is Tricky

So why do siblings have the will to fight? Partly because there is a natural competition for shared family resources, parental attention, and parental approval. When parents appear to play favorites in response, the seeds for rivalry between adult siblings can be sown. "My parents always liked my sister better than me when we were children, and now that we're grown up, they still do. She can do no wrong in their eyes, and whatever I do is never good enough!" Favoritism is family discrimination, and it intensifies sibling rivalry with resentment, the less favored child taking anger out on the favored sibling for what parents have unfairly done.

A BETTER PARENTING PRACTICE

More powerful than getting angry to stop children from hitting each other, you might try this: "I appreciate how well you both usually get along. When you start hitting, I feel sad that you would want to hurt each other, because I want our family to be free of deliberate harm." Get mad at them and they become defensive. Feel sad for them and they may respond to your concern.

For most siblings, however, there is plenty to fight about even without parental favoritism. Siblings typically engage in conflict:

- To test power (Who is dominant?)
- To establish individuality (Who is different?)

- To ventilate emotions (Who needs to relieve a bad mood?)

What is satisfying for siblings, however, can be exhausting for parents. The children's conflict is one more unwelcome source of stress in the parents' stressful world. It can feel unpleasant, irritating, and upsetting. In response, the parents' attitude can be affected. They become more negative, they become more fatigued, they become more prone to getting into conflict with each other, and they have less positive energy to give to other children who were not party to the conflict to begin with.

The Parental Role in Sibling Conflict

Parents have four roles in dealing with sibling conflict. They act as separator, keeping children apart to reduce fighting and the stress it causes parents. They act as monitor, making sure that conflict is conducted within safe limits so neither party gets hurt or feels abused. They act as governor, intervening to control the conflict when it is threatening to escalate to harmful effect. And they act as mediator, settling differences the children are unable to settle themselves.

A BETTER PARENTING PRACTICE

The phrase "I hate you!" has no place in family conflict. Hatred justifies treating other people with the worst hurt one has to give. If a child uses the phrase, tell him that you would rather hear "I am completely angry at you!" Then take time to talk the anger out.

Because conflict is cooperative, parents must never get sucked into the trap of figuring out who started the fight in order to punish the guilty party. If they try to determine who started the conflict, they will go back to year one. Since it takes two parties to create a conflict, hold both siblings cooperatively responsible. You can try and mediate the conflict if you choose, but remember the saying, "Blessed be the mediator, for he shall be hated by both sides." Because your solution will give the children less than 100 percent of what each wants, both will consider your resolution unfair. "Just because we couldn't agree over which TV show to watch, now you've decided we don't get to watch TV tonight at all!" Or you may just separate the combatants for a prescribed cooling off period for them, and a rest for you.

Mediate or separate; however, you must hold each sibling accountable for individual behavior in the conflict. "You need to know that, although I hold you both responsible for creating any conflict between you, I hold you separately responsible for how you treat each other during the conflict. If either of you acts in deliberately hurtful ways, then that person is going to have some business with me. You will conduct your disagreements with each other safely because safety is the rule for conflict that everyone in this family is expected to follow. Do you understand?"

Chapter 10

What if Your One and Only Child Is Willful?

Ten Things You Will Learn in This Chapter

- Why being the parent of an only child is considered "high-pressure" parenting.

- How peer pressure is very different for only children.

- Why being the sole focus of your attention can give your child too much power.

- About the negative affects of overparenting and how to avoid it.

- Some common examples of overparenting.

- How the pressure you put on yourself will translate onto your child.

- That you need to be careful what lessons you may be teaching your child without even knowing it.

- How socializing is SO important for your only child—and you!

- What is in your control and what is not—and how to handle both.

- What "being mature beyond his/her years" really means.

Fixing Your Family Dynamics?

Since the baby boom of the 1950s, families in the United States have been growing smaller. Today, somewhere between 20 and 30 percent of dual- and single-parent families have an only child. Because of family dynamics, there are tendencies (not certainties) that favor a high degree of willfulness developing in an only child: from the adult tendency to overparent, from the child's tendency to become demanding, from the child's tendency to become controlling or rigid, from the child's tendency to become precocious, and from the child's experience with adolescence.

Whatever the cause or choice, only-child families are subject to certain dynamics that multiple-child families are not. When all parental attention is concentrated on a single child, when this single child has no sibling to distract the parents' unsparing gaze, when their first child is the only chance to parent that parents are going to get, predictable pressures build. Contrary to the common assumption that single-child families are less complex and demanding to manage than multiple-child families, raising an only child is high-pressure parenting. With one offspring, the performance stakes for parents and child can feel extremely high, with both parties intensely emotionally sensitized and committed to each other's well-being.

Pressure on the Parents

For the parents, there is pressure from knowing that this is first and last child in one, the only chance at parenting they get, and so they want to make the most of their parenting experience by doing their best, by doing it "right." They want their child to "turn out well." And they definitely do not want to do it "wrong" by making decisions that in some way harm their beloved child. This conscientiousness makes for extremely thoughtful and labor-intensive parenting. One common outcome of this thoughtfulness is a clear and firm agenda about what they want for the child, set ideas for what they should provide and how their child should perform. Most parents of an only child do not parent by lying back and playing wait and see. They take initiative because parents of an only child usually have a will of their own.

DID YOU KNOW?

Two times in life when being "only" can be costly are marriage and parental end-care. When only children marry, they usually have to learn to do more sharing, adjust to more differences, and constructively resolve more conflicts than they have been accustomed to doing before. And when their parents are in age decline (or in medical emergency), they are the only offspring, with no sibling support, available or expected to help.

Pressure on the Child

For the child, there is no push and shove; no rough and tumble; no conflicts over dominance, differences, attention, or sharing with siblings. Nor are there child companions in the family to play with, with whom one can get additional perceptions of parents to put them into more realistic perspective. There are only adults for family company, and the child is ruled by desire to please these powers that be, to fit in to their company, to imitate their ways. When parents are one's only peers at home, peer pressure to belong can be intense.

Pressure on the Relationship

As for the relationship between parents and only child, it is extremely close and knowledgeable and sensitive, often emotionally enmeshed, where unhappiness in one party stimulates unhappiness in the other, who often feels responsible for fixing the problem so everyone's well-being can be restored. They take great pleasure in each other's company, creating a mutual admiration society. To preserve that association, a tyranny of pleasing can be established, with parents hating to upset their child and the child hating to offend or disappoint his or her parents.

Being the sole focus of parental attention, the only child occupies a powerful position in the family, and that power is the foundation of the willfulness that most only children develop.

The Dangers of Overparenting

Most only children are very well parented. They are well attached, well loved, and well supervised; their interests and capacities are well developed; they are well self-connected (knowing how to keep themselves good company); and they know what parents expect of them. But a major contributor to an only child's willfulness can be the varieties of overparenting that parents give. Wanting to do well by their one and only child can make it hard for parents to moderate their efforts and easy to err on the side of pushing themselves too hard and pushing their child hard as a result. Overparenting is simply carrying a certain focus of concern to such an extreme degree that the child is extremely affected as a result, becoming more willful in a certain way. This interaction takes an infinite variety of forms.

Common Types of Overparenting

Consider just a few overparenting interactions and the variety of ways an only child's willfulness can be enhanced.

- In response to oversensitive parents, an only child can become extremely vulnerable.
- In response to overdependent parents, an only child can become extremely obligated.
- In response to overambitious parents, an only child can become extremely driven.
- In response to overprotective parents, an only child can become extremely cautious.
- In response to overwatchful parents, an only child can become extremely self-conscious.
- In response to overcontrolling parents, an only child can become extremely passive.
- In response to overindulgent parents, an only child can become extremely entitled.

- In response to overpraising parents, an only child can become extremely arrogant.
- In response to overpermissive parents, an only child can become extremely selfish.
- In response to overstrict parents, an only child can become extremely rigid.
- In response to overanxious parents, an only child can become extremely fearful.

If parents are feeling uncertain about whether to make more or less parenting effort for their only child, because of this tendency to overparent, doing less may be the better choice. As one only child put it, "I wish I wasn't all my parents had to do!"

Guarding Against Extreme Concern

Wanting to parent extremely well can drive overdedicated mothers and fathers to extreme behaviors out of extreme concern, often provoking an extreme response in their only child, who becomes extremely willful in that regard. Therefore, it is usually best for parents of an only child to relax their concern and moderate their efforts. In most cases, if they halved their parenting dedication, they'd probably do twice as much as many parents with larger families who have learned that turning in a mixed performance, and paying some attention (not all), provides enough quality of care for most children to come out okay.

The lesson is simply this: pressure translates. You can't apply a lot of pressure on your own parenting performance without putting a lot of pressure on your only child. If you demand perfection of yourself as a parent, exhibiting no tolerance for your own frailties and misjudgments, your child will learn to do the same. Why? Because with no siblings to display contrasting traits, with whom to develop contrasting relationships, and with no one in the home but parents to identify with, an only child is highly encouraged to resemble parents, who often reward acts of similarity: "Good for you, you did it just like us!"

DID YOU KNOW

Since family forces of similarity greatly amplify pressure on the only child to believe and behave like her parents, be mindful and moderate in your treatment of yourself for the sake of your child. How willfully hard you are on yourselves is how willfully hard your only child is likely to be on herself.

Not only does your child unconsciously copy you, adopting your attitudes and other traits unawares, but he or she also consciously imitates you, out of admiration for you, identification with you, and in search of approval from you. And, of course, the child also learns to live like you by being expected to live according to the family terms you set.

Is Your Child Demanding and Controlling Only?

From having parents who strive to please their only child, that child can learn to become demanding. From having parents who worry lest their only child come to harm and want that child to turn out "right," controlling parents can teach their child to value high control. Becoming highly demanding and highly controlling makes for a very willful only child.

The issues of demand and control need to be separated. Demanding is a unilateral act—one person can do it unassisted. Controlling, however, requires the consent of others. With their only child, parents need to address both issues.

The Demanding Only Child

Being the exclusive focus of so much parental attention and support, it is hard for many only children not to grow up with a sense of entitlement:

- "If I want it, I should get it."
- "If I have something to say, people should listen to me."
- "If I feel I am right, others should agree with me."
- "If I don't like how others are treating me, they should be made to stop."
- "If I have a way of doing things, others should go along."

To the degree an only child subscribes to any of these beliefs, he can be quite demanding to live with, to play with, and to teach. Unhappily, even parents can grow weary of this tyranny of demand, finding their beloved child grown self-centered to his cost. "Me first!" "Me only!" "Me now!" What about anybody else? Indeed.

So parents need to socialize their only child to understand that functional relationships need to work for two parties, not just one. Hence, they teach the three principles of mutuality (also discussed in Chapter 2):

- **Reciprocity:** "Just as we do for you, we expect you to do for us."
- **Consideration:** "Just as we show sensitivity for your well-being, we expect you to show sensitivity for ours."
- **Compromise:** "Just as we sacrifice some self-interest to meet you halfway, we expect you to do the same with us."

Parents of a young only child who has not been taught to live by the principles of mutuality can pay a heavy price once the child reaches adolescence and naturally becomes more demanding in pursuit of his or her independence. The lesson is, start this instruction early or pay for that lack of education later on.

The Controlling Only Child

The controlling child problem is usually the compliant parent problem. Out of the desire to please, the fear of disapproval, the discomfort with conflict, or the inability to set limits, these parents:

- Give in when they would rather refuse.
- Go along with what they don't agree with.
- Say yes when they wish they could say no.
- Accept conduct they know is unacceptable.

- Adjust to treatment they know is unhealthy.
- Rescue the child from the unhappy consequences of unwise decisions.

All of these choices are in the parents' control, not the child's. So who's got the problem? Extremely indulgent parents can be guilty of extreme neglect—neglecting their parental responsibility to make healthy demands on their child. The controlling only child is being spoiled for later relationships by learning within family that others should always give that child her way and that rules for social conduct that apply to others do not apply to her.

Overly compliant parents must consider two notions. First, parenting is not a popularity contest. It is a tough process of preparation for learning the necessary skills for adult independence. And second, one responsibility parents have is to socialize their child to be nice to live with at home so he or she doesn't need to "control" relationships to get along with others later on.

Intolerance for Being in the Wrong

One of the great pleasures of having an only child is the pleasure parents and child enjoy giving to each other. Both want to please, both want to do right by each other. Conversely, to wrong, to do wrong, or to be in the wrong can court disappointment and disapproval that can be hard to bear. "I can't stand letting my parents down!" "We just hate having our child have to pay for our mistakes!"

This desire to please can be dangerous when it sows the seed of perfectionism—the need to be right and do right all the time. Perfectionism sets an unrealistic expectation because "to err is human," to be ideal is not. The only way to be perfect parents is to have a perfectly behaving child, and who would want to put that kind of pressure on a beloved only child?

DID YOU KNOW?

The primary influence of parents is not in what they say but in what they model. It is through how they treat themselves, other people, and the world that they instruct the child how to act. Parents who cannot tolerate admitting wrong in themselves are at risk of instilling that same intolerance in their only child.

In the normal course of growing through their son's or daughter's childhood together, both parents and only child will have misadventures, make mistakes, and commit misdeeds that put them each for the moment in the wrong. Unless this expectation is clearly communicated by parents, unless they are willing to admit their own wrongs, apologize, make amends, forgive themselves, and go forward, the only child will have a hard time tolerating being in the wrong when his time comes. Unless they can let go of hard feelings when the child has done wrong, the inevitability of her occasional wrongdoing will never feel safe.

The Power of Being Precocious

Another contributor to becoming adultized, in addition to similarity training, is early enfranchisement. Although the social voting age is eighteen for most young people, for an only child, the family "voting age" is much younger. He is often given equal say and influence in determining family activities: "What do you think we should do?"

DID YOU KNOW?

There's nothing wrong in empowering the only child by including and involving her in adult decision making, but the more "votes" parents give their only child in determining the conduct of family affairs, the more willful that child shall become.

In cases of extremely precocious development, friends of the parents may notice how the child acts mature beyond her years, praising her for this speed of social development. "She acts so much older than other children her age!" No wonder they're impressed. She has become more conversant with the culture and world of her parents than with the culture and world of children her own age.

Acting More Grown Up

Only children are at risk of growing so verbally and socially precocious that they can have difficulty fitting in and making friends with a group of other children the same age. Such only children are more at ease with adults (with whom they can comfortably communicate and relate) and with younger children (with whom they can be socially in charge). This is why parents of an only child must arrange for adequate socializing outside of parental, and parental friend, company so the boy or girl can learn to enjoy interacting with same-age peers. Possessive parents who are reluctant to share the pleasure of their only child with anyone else only retard the social learning with peers that she needs to accomplish.

DOES THIS SOUND LIKE YOUR CHILD?

To the degree that only children are lonely, it is usually not a function of being the only child at home, but rather because they feel precociously out of step with same-age peers and become socially ill at ease or even isolated on that account.

One benefit of being adultized is that the only child is not shy about talking with adults; she is precociously skilled in expressing her needs and negotiating her way with these older people who control so many parts of her world. Assuming adultlike standing with her parents, she is not intimidated by their or other adult authority. Willful in this regard, she may consider herself the equal of any adult and therefore entitled to challenge other adult authority with which she disagrees. "When I don't agree with what you want me to do at home, I tell you and we work something out, so why shouldn't I be able to do the same with my teacher at school?" As for the teacher, she may see the need to cut the presumptuous young student down to child size. "In this classroom, I make the rules, and your job is to obey, not to question why." Sometimes willfulness with external authority can get the only child in trouble.

Chapter 11

Keep Your Emotions in Check

Ten Things You Will Learn in This Chapter

- What "emotional loading" is and how to avoid it.

- How it's important to give your child adequate space and time to calm down.

- Why emotions are good and bad and how to harness them—and teach your child to too.

- To learn to perceive and interpret your child's actions in a positive manner.

- About drugs and alcohol and the dangerous connection with strong-willed people.

- Whether or not you are an anger-prone parent.

- How to channel your anger effectively and make it functional.

- To avoid resentment and let go of hurt feelings— and how to teach this tough lesson to your kids.

- About temper tantrums—how to act, what they mean, how to avoid them.

- Two ways to control your emotions and keep them from escalating.

When Your Emotions Run High

Emotions can be intense in a family with a strong-willed child. Everyone in the family is affected by the willful child in a variety of ways, and often they let high emotion get in the way of effective decision making. Making the right decisions about how to behave, how to respond, how to react, and how to teach your willful child is best done when you are thinking rationally, not emotionally.

A BETTER PARENTING PRACTICE

Beware emotional loading—labeling objectionable behavior with insulting, inflammatory language. When parents angrily call their four-year-old, who has regressed to thumb sucking, a "baby" for act-ing infantile, this only increases the emotional power of the interaction. The label offends the child and upsets the parents, perhaps encouraging the willful child to act "baby" with a vengeance, crying for a bottle and maybe breaking toilet training, too, making a hard situation worse.

Emotions can run high in a family where there is a strong-willed child, because upset is so easy to come by for everyone concerned. Siblings of the strong-willed child can resent how much attention their willful sib-ling gets and the exceptions to family rules she seems to get away with. Parents can grow weary and become impatient keeping up with the child's demands and contending with her resistance. And the willful child can bridle with frustration against parental restraints that stand in the way of what she intensely wants to do. Maintaining an unemotional stance is important in being effective and exerting positive influence over your strong-willed child.

When the willful child becomes intensely emotional, for a short while there is no thinking person home. This is not the time for parents to jam the child with a demand to declare what is going on. Lost in the emotional moment, the child may not know what is really going on. Instead, give her time and space to calm down, to restore thought, to identify what she is feeling so it can be safely and productively talked out. When the child says, "I need to think about what I'm feeling," she isn't lying. For the willful child, feelings are often confusing, and he or she needs time to figure them out.

Emotions Are Your Friend and Foe

As consistently as you can, maintain your emotional sobriety: Keep calm and stay cool and be reasonable, and help your willful child learn to do the same. If you start "thinking" with your feelings, you will make poor decisions. Emotions are good informants but bad advisors. As informants they alert us to what is going on. Fear alerts us to dangers. Frustration alerts us to obstructions. Anger alerts us to violations. But as advisors, emotions can make matters worse, not better. Fear can advise us to run from what is scary, rather than face it. Frustration can advise us to force a situation, rather than be patient. Anger can advise us to retaliate, rather than negotiate. Emotion is for sensing what is going on; thought is for deciding what to do.

It is the parent's job to teach the willful child to separate the functions of emotion and thought. For example, hurt and angry from being teased, the willful child vows to never play with his best friends again. To which the parent responds, "First tell me all about what happened and how you feel; then afterward, we can think together about what is wise to do."

Thought Mediates Emotion

How you interpret what happens to you is often more important than the happening itself. Imagine a middle-school-age girl who has just lost her best friend of many years because early adolescence has caused the two young girls to grow their separate ways, to grow apart. Now her best friend wants different friends instead. Knowing that her daughter is suffering because of this loss of intimate companionship on which she has relied for many years, the parent attends very carefully to the interpretation her unhappy daughter puts on this adverse event.

Will her daughter say, "This just goes to show what a loser I am! Nobody could like someone like me! I'll never have a friend again!" Or will her daughter say, "This really hurts to lose my friend. She wanted a change, but not because there's something wrong with me. In fact, having had a best friend just shows that I'll be able to make another good friend again."

The first interpretation leads to insecurity, low self-esteem, and despair. The second interpretation can lead to confidence, self-assurance, and hope. If this were your daughter, which interpretation would you want her to make? The lesson for parents is this: Attend to your child's perceptions about what is happening in life and her interpretations about what those happenings mean. How she chooses to think affects how she is going to feel.

Dire interpretations of adverse events are dangerous because they can drive exhausted parents or willful child to emotional extremes. When either parents or child are becoming upset, they need to ask themselves, "What am I thinking?" To change how they feel, they can change how they think. Instead of assuming, "You did that on purpose," the parent or child could choose to suppose, "You did that by mistake."

Objective and Subjective Responses

Or consider a casual interaction between parent and willful child at the end of the school day. You ask your child for household help as he passes you on the stairs, and he appears to ignore your request. What do you choose to think about that response? You could choose to take it personally and make a subjective response: "He just treated me rudely by not responding. That makes me really angry. I'm going to let him know I don't like it!" Or you could choose to take it impersonally and make an objective response: "He didn't reply to my request; I need to ask again for what I need."

How people perceive and interpret what is going on makes an enormous difference in how people respond to each other emotionally. The more realistic, operational, and objective your thinking is, the less emotionally upset you are likely to become. The more evaluative, distorted, and subjective your thinking is, the more emotionally intense your family interactions are likely to be.

DID YOU KNOW

Both alcohol and drug use can affect a person's mental attitude and emotional sobriety. Parents who get mean when they drink at the end of the day often do so because, under the influence, they get in a mood to review grievances or decide to perceive themselves as treated unjustly. Then they start looking to provoke a fight so they can retaliate and feel better.

So when your willful child enters adolescence and discloses less to you and more to peers, which interpretation of this changed behavior do you choose to make? "She is more private now than as a child, needs more separation from her parents, and would rather confide in friends." Make this interpretation and you will feel calm and accepting, maintain perspective, and stay available to your less communicative teenager. Or do you choose a different interpretation? "She is rejecting our relationship, doesn't love me anymore, and is trying to make me feel bad." Feeling hurt and angry by choosing to think like this, the parent may punish back and push her daughter further away. Such gloomy thinking can cause painful feelings that can motivate a negative response.

How to Take Responsibilities

"She makes me so angry!" storms a parent when describing her willful child. But this is untrue. The parent is responsible for her own feelings. If her child can make her angry, then the child is controlling her emotions. And letting your child control your emotions means giving away a lot of power. People often externalize the cause of their anger with blame: "That made me angry." "You made me angry." Only by internalizing the source of our anger—"I am choosing to feel angry because of how you treated me"—can we keep it under responsible control.

The Anger-Prone Parent

There is a type of parent who is sure his anger is everybody else's fault: the anger-prone parent. "Well, if the kids would just do what they're told, I wouldn't get mad!" "Well, if the kids just did things correctly, I wouldn't get mad!" "Well, if the kids wouldn't deliberately provoke me, I wouldn't get mad!" The anger-prone parent is willful in three potentially damaging ways.

- He has a high need for control. He has to get his way and gets mad when he does not.
- He is highly judgmental. He believes he knows what's right and gets mad when others do or see things incorrectly in his estimation.
- He is highly sensitive to insult. He takes personally what is not personally intended, getting mad because he believes others are deliberately out to upset him.

Combine in the same family an anger-prone parent with a willful child, and there is potential for an emotional explosion every time the child challenges or resists parental authority or a conflict of interests occurs. To anger-prone parents, there are no small offenses or disagreements, because each can contribute to an abiding sense of grievance: "Something is always going wrong!"

DID YOU KNOW?

One sure formula for creating unceasing power struggles in a family is pairing a willful child with an anger-prone parent. If, as the parent, you want to change the formula, then you have to change yourself.

For the willful child, anger-prone parents teach a constant lesson that not getting what one wants merits becoming angry. Anger-prone parents, by example and interaction, train their willful child to become anger-prone in response. "I learned my temper from my father. When things didn't go the way he wanted, the first thing he did was blow up about it. Now I'm the same way."

Fortunately, if anger-prone parents want to change their volatile ways, they can. This change requires ceasing to blame the object of their anger for their anger, and reclaiming responsibility for their own emotions. They can choose to change their emotional set points by altering beliefs that justify an angry response.

- To become less controlling, they can practice saying to themselves, "I don't need to get my way all the time."
- To become less judgmental, they can practice saying to themselves, "I don't have to be right all the time."
- To take events less personally, they can say to themselves, "I don't have to assume that actions I don't like are deliberately meant to upset me."

Anger Interferes with Two-Step Thinking

Anger-prone adults are prone to one-step thinking, because when angry, they tend to become ruled by impulse, feeling, and the need for immediate gratification. Anger makes two-step thinking more difficult to do. Anger makes it hard to delay action and consult judgment (what is reasonable, ethical, and wise) before making a decision.

When the recovering anger-prone parent is able to change his emotional set points and engage in two-step thinking, the results can be pretty dramatic.

My daughter took my camera without asking and returned it broken, excusing what she did by saying that I never said she couldn't borrow it, and it was old and falling apart anyhow. Well, I was all set to go off on her when I realized that was what she had come to expect. I'd blow up and then she'd blow up and that would take the place of dealing with the offense. So I took the time to stop and think, and decided to violate her prediction. In this calm voice, I matter-of-factly explained that taking my things without permission was theft, that I felt disrespected, and that stealing was not allowed. And for breaking the camera, she would have to pay to get it repaired. No blow up. Just feedback, rule setting, and consequence. Without my anger, she could hear what I had to say and could agree to do as I asked.

A second-step statement got a second-step response. The parent in this case put into practice the understanding that people only get as angry as they want to, as they think they should, as they choose.

How Can Anger Help You?

Anger, like any emotion, is functional. The purpose of anger is to identify violations to our well-being. "You took what was mine!" "You hurt me on purpose!" "You broke your promise!" "You shouldn't have done that!" The angry person feels wronged, that he or she was mistreated, that he or she was dealt with unfairly. Anger helps adults and children identify these kinds of violations.

After anger identifies a violation of our well-being, it can then empower us to make an expressive response ("That hurt!"), a protective response ("You shouldn't do that!"), a corrective response ("Don't do that again!"), or all three.

Since anger can be a dangerous emotion when it motivates aggressive (control-taking) behavior in response, children must be taught nondestructive ways to manage anger. When a child's sibling takes a toy from him and the child then gets into a hitting fight with him to get it back, parents intervene. They try to help the warring children move from acting out to talking out to working out their conflict. To this end, parents declare a time-out to stop the acting out, to create a break to calm emotions down so talking out and then working out can occur.

A BETTER PARENTING PRACTICE

If your spouse and children say your facial expression is scary when you get very angry and you don't believe them, check it out. Next time you feel in a rage, go look in a mirror and see what the rest of the family is talking about. Maybe you wouldn't like to be around a person that looked so angry, either.

Willful children, because they are so easily frustrated, are at risk of becoming prone to anger. "I get mad when I can't get what I want or do what I want or have to do what I don't want!" When parents question the child's right to anger now, the child is likely to get angrier later on. Parental responses such as "You shouldn't be angry" or "That's no reason to get angry" only discourage the child from talking anger out and increase the likelihood of shutting up, building up, and blowing up when the accumulation of unexpressed anger can no longer be contained.

By example and instruction, parents need to discuss with their willful child the nature and management of anger. At a relaxed time—not an upset time—they can choose to raise some of the seven talking points about anger listed here.

- You can become angry when you decide that something has been done to you that you believe should not have happened.
- Your anger is not involuntary; it is a matter of your personal choice. How you think about what happened is what makes you angry, not what another person did.
- No one can make you angry without your permission.
- Blaming someone for making you angry only shows that you have given control of your anger to that person. This is not a good idea.
- Take responsibility for deciding to get angry and we can use that emotional energy to make an expressive, protective, or corrective response.
- Anger is always an expression of caring. People don't get angry at what doesn't matter to them.

When you decide to get angry, ask yourself what you really care about in this situation, then discuss with the other person what matters to you about what just happened, why you need it to stop, and see what you can do to work it out.

Watch Emotional Escalation
Two common ways that parents and willful child can escalate emotion between them are when parents get

into yelling cycles and when the willful child throws temper tantrums. Parents need to know how to reduce the likelihood of both events.

Yelling Cycles

Parental yelling is usually an expression of frustration with their willful child's repeated delay to do what they asked or to stop doing what they forbid. They didn't start out yelling, but they ended up that way, and the more often they have to get to the yelling point to get compliance, the sooner they get to yelling the next time around.

A BETTER PARENTING PRACTICE

Don't hold on to hurt feelings. The longer you do, the more resentful you will become. Keep in mind the adage from Alcoholics Anonymous: "Resentment is like taking poison and waiting for the other person to die." Your hostility may be offensive to others, but you are mostly "poisoning" yourself.

Parental yelling is definitely a loss of emotional sobriety. It shows the child how delay can successfully provoke parental upset, and it shows the child that parents have reached the point where they are finally serious about what they asked. This is how yelling cycles work: now the child waits to be yelled at before complying, while parents yell when fed up with the delay.

Parents who yell place their faith in increased volume of speech: "The louder I speak, the more I can force you to hear and obey what I have to say." Parents believe that they are talking out when they yell, but they are not. They are acting out frustration and training their child to delay compliance until parents have reached the high frustration point. This is how yelling cycles are learned. Yelling is counterproductive for at least four reasons.

- The child who is yelled at can feel angry, hurt, or frightened as the yelling parent causes the relationship to feel unsafe.
- The message parents want to send is obscured by the intensity and volume of frustration and anger they express.
- By modeling yelling, parents often encourage the child to yell back in return.
- The parents have lost control to get control, and the child ends up in control by being given this emotionally provocative power.

Stopping a yelling cycle is very simple: stop yelling to get what you want. Calmly and insistently pursue what you want with supervision or exchange points (see Chapter 8). Some parents who are recovering from being yellers find going to the other extreme to be very effective. They actually talk more softly. Not only does the child not predict this response, but he now has to listen carefully to hear what is being said. And now a new cue for parental seriousness is created: "I know my mom really means business when she lowers her voice."

Temper Tantrums

A temper tantrum is equal parts an intense expression of frustration or hurt, an increased emotional clamor to attract attention, and a calculated manipulation to get one's way. The willful four-year-old who is head banging and screaming on the floor in protest of parents' denying what he wants is sincerely upset. He is also creating a clamor to command parental attention. And he is using upset, loudness, and acting out to try and change their mind. Because a tantrum is part honest expression of emotion (some mix of suffering and anger), parents should try to hear the feelings out, but they must insist on civil communication and they must not give the episode any extortionate power. How can you do this?

- To the expression of discomfort or hurt, make an empathetic response: "You are feeling really upset; please tell me about it, I want to know."
- To the use of clamor to attract attention, make a limiting response: "When you yell, I can't hear you for all the noise; if you want me to listen, you must calm down and speak quietly."
- To the acting out of suffering and anger to get one's way, make a negating response: "No matter how extremely unhappy you act, that is not going to change my mind."

Some people advise parents to ignore a temper tantrum and let the child rage and cry out her upset. It's better to respond to the tantrum with empathetic, limiting, and negating responses because of good lessons those responses have to teach: to learn to talk out emotion, to learn to do so in a calm and civil manner, and to forsake using intense emotionality for manipulative gain. To help a child recover from a tantrum, first ask, "Tell me what you feel; I want to hear." Second ask, "Tell me what you think; I want to understand." Third ask, "Tell me what you need; I want to know." Fourth ask, "Tell me what you could do, now that you can't have what you wanted, to feel better. Maybe I can help."

Avoid Overractions

For both parent and willful child, sometime it's bound to happen: someone overreacts emotionally. For no apparent good cause, usually in response to something too small to merit such an intense response, either party will explode in upset, and the other will wonder "What's going on?" Even the overreactor may be puzzled: "Why did such a minor event set me off?"

So the other person didn't hear what you said; so what? So the other person didn't show up exactly on time; so what? So the other person mentioned what you said to somebody else; so what? Little things shouldn't cause such major upsets, you may believe. Oh, yes, they often should. And both parties need to understand why, to profit from that understanding.

Little Things Are Big Things in Disguise

When a little event sets off a disproportionately large emotional reaction for you or your willful child, you know that the small happening was really a "big thing" in disguise. The person who explodes is amplifying the significance of a small event into an emotional reaction for a number of common causes—from stress, from suppression, from symbolism, from similarity, or from surprise.

DID YOU KNOW?

The most important skill for parent and willful child to learn in their relationship is self-calming techniques to preserve emotional sobriety. Use strategies for interrupting emotional intensity to bring down emotion levels when you get frustrated with each other. These strategies will help prevent feelings from overwhelming thinking when disagreement occurs.

Already exhausted from overdemand at work, one small additional thing to do at home is enough to carry you over your emotional tipping point and you explode. "I've been cleaning up after people all day at work, so wash those snack dishes in the sink, and I mean now!" Overreactions from stress are usually a result of exhaustion.

Having spent a whole day at school being teased and saying nothing back, your child explodes at you for criticizing her messy room. "Why don't you just get in line with all the other people who don't like me. Now leave me alone!" Overreactions from suppression are usually the result of emotional buildup from unexpressed irritations, insults, or injuries.

Waiting for your spouse to arrive an hour late without calling, you explode when he finally walks in the door. "Not calling when you knew you were going to be late just goes to show how you never consider my feelings!" Symbolic overreactions are usually the result of what specific actions come to signify and represent.

Giving the first child home from school first chance to play with the new computer infuriates the older child when he gets home from sports. "This is just like what has happened a million times since she was born. My younger sister gets favored over me!" Similarity overreactions are usually the result of a current occurrence that reminds someone of something painful that has happened before.

You did not think to tell your child that your weekend plans have changed and you won't be able to provide transportation she assumed would be available; she reacts like she's been betrayed. "You never tell me anything! I'm just left to find stuff out at the last minute, when it's going to mess up my life!" Overreactions from surprise are usually from an unexpected turn of events that prove disruptive.

What Overreactions Can Teach

Although at the time overreactions command a lot of attention, once over, they tend to be ignored. People just want to forget the unpleasantness and put it behind them. The person who overreacted feels foolish for having blown up at something so small, and the person blown up at doesn't want to revisit the discomfort. This immediate dismissal of an unhappy event, however, is a mistake. Overreactions can be very informative if people will take the time to learn from what hidden issues have to teach. Understand the reasons behind the other person's unreasonable behavior, or your own, and you can gain valuable insight. Do this by asking clarifying questions that can unlock what is really going on.

- Ask the stress question: "Have you experienced a lot of other demands today?"
- Ask the suppression question: "Has there been another hard experience upsetting you?"
- Ask the symbolism question: "What does how I just acted represent to you?"
- Ask the similarity question: "What does what happened remind you of?"
- Ask the surprise question: "What were you thinking would occur?"

It is a wasted opportunity to let emotional overreactions go. Use clarifying questions to tease the meaning out. Although both parent and willful child might wish the episode had never happened, since it did, learn from it all you can.

Willpower to the Rescue

At the outset of this book, willfulness was presented in a positive light. It is appropriate to end this book with that emphasis now. To safeguard your child from substance problems, parenting to encourage a certain kind of willfulness is an extremely powerful preventative, the will to engage with normal challenges of growing up. If you will train your child to develop this willfulness, you reduce her susceptibility to substance use and abuse.

The Nine Wills for Engagement

Growing up poses many challenges. It takes a strong will to engage these challenges and to acquire the life skills each has to teach. When these skills are learned, healthy growth is enhanced. When these skills are not learned, which often happens with the substance using and abusing child, disengagement from challenge retards healthy growth.

So compare two seventeen-year-olds from comparable backgrounds and experiences who are different in this regard. Child #1 has remained substance-free. Child #2 has been using substances since age thirteen:

- When it comes to meeting the challenge of commitment, #1 has developed the will to keep promises to self and others, but #2 has disengaged and routinely breaks promises to self and others.
- When it comes to meeting the challenge of completion, #1 has developed the will to finish what is started, but #2 has disengaged and routinely doesn't finish what is started.
- When it comes to meeting the challenge of consistency, #1 has developed the will to maintain continuity of effort, but #2 has disengaged and routinely doesn't maintain ongoing effort.
- When it comes to meeting the challenge of confrontation, #1 has developed the will to encounter

painful situations, but #2 has disengaged and routinely avoids dealing with painful situations.

- When it comes to meeting the challenge of control, #1 has developed the will to let judgment rule over impulse, but #2 has disengaged and routinely lets impulse rule over judgment.
- When it comes to meeting the challenge of consequences, #1 has developed the will to own the results of actions taken, but #2 has disengaged and routinely disowns results of actions taken.
- When it comes to meeting the challenge of closure, #1 has developed the will to decide by hard choice when deciding gets hard, but #2 has disengaged and routinely decides by default, letting circumstance decide when choice gets hard.
- When it comes to meeting the challenge of communication, #1 has developed the will to speak up about and talk out hard feelings, but #2 has disengaged and routinely shuts up about or acts out hard feelings.
- When it comes to meeting the challenge of caring, #1 has developed the will to hold on to what he or she deeply believes and what has traditionally mattered, but #2 has disengaged and routinely betrays deep beliefs and what has traditionally mattered.

Without benefit of a strong will, notice what attributes substance-using child #2 sacrifices. By breaking promises to self and others, the child has lost some faith in his or her capacity for self-reliance. By repeatedly starting much but finishing little, the child has lost some confidence in his or her capacity to follow through and meet personal goals. By repeatedly being unable to keep up a healthy daily regimen, the child has lost some capacity for self-care. By repeatedly choosing to escape personal pain, the child has lost some capacity to tolerate and talk out emotional hurt. By repeatedly giving in to the lure of immediate gratification, the child has lost some capacity to resist temptation. By repeatedly denying the connection between bad choice and bad consequence, the child has lost some capacity for assuming personal responsibility. By repeatedly letting circumstance determine difficult decisions, the child has lost some capacity for mental toughness. By repeatedly refusing to express hard feelings directly, the child has lost some capacity for open and honest communication. By repeatedly betraying deep beliefs and what has traditionally mattered, the child has lost some capacity to maintain personal integrity.

APPENDIX A

Helpful Websites

For monthly articles about parenting by author/psychologist Carl Pickhardt Ph.D.:

www.carlpickhardt.com

For articles to support healthy parenting from the American Academy of Pediatrics:

www.aap.org

For guidance to effective drug treatment programs:

www.drugstrategies.com

For information about parenting an only child:

www.onlychild.com

For information about single parenting:

www.parentswithoutpartners.com

For information about a wide range of parenting topics:

www.familyeducation.com

For information about positive discipline:

www.parenttrainingcenter.com

For research-based information about parenting:

www.npin.org

For information about effective parenting:
www.parenting-ed.org

For information from a variety of parenting experts:
www.tnpc.com

For information about child-care, health care, and media
impact:
www.thekidsshow.org

For information about positive parenting:
www.positiveparenting.com

For Canadian-based information across many areas of
parenting concern:
www.eparentingnetwork.com

For information about positive discipline up to age twelve:
www.pocketparent.com

For information about parenting adolescents:
www.thesuccessfulparent.com

For information from dialoguing with other parents:
www.parents-talk.com

APPENDIX B

Helpful Books

Pickhardt, Carl, Ph.D. *The Everything® Parent's Guide to Positive Discipline* (Avon, MA: Adams Media Corporation, 2004).

Pickhardt, Carl, Ph.D. *Keys to Successful Stepfathering* (New York: Barron's, 1997).

Forehand, Rex L. *Parenting the Strong-Willed Child.* (NTC Publishing Group: Lincolnwood, IL, 1996).

MacKenzie, Robert J. *Setting Limits with Your Strong-Willed Child.* (New York: Crown Publishing, 2001).

Dobson, James C. Ph.D. *The Strong-Willed Child.* (Carol Stream, IL: Tyndale House Publishers, 1997).

Smiley, Kendra. *Aaron's Way: The Journey of a Strong-Willed Child.* (Chicago, IL: Moody Press, 2004).

Barkley, Russell A. *Your Defiant Child—Eight Steps to Better Behavior.* (New York: The Guilford Press, 1998).

Reynolds, Randy. *Good News About Your Strong-Willed Child.* (Grand Rapids, MI: Zondervan, 1995)

Pickhardt, C. E. *The Case of the Scary Divorce – A Jackson Skye Mystery* (Washington, DC: Magination Press, The American Psychological Association, 1997).

APPENDIX C

Helpful Support Groups

PARENTS ANONYMOUS, for strengthening families, breaking the cycle of abuse, and helping parents create safe homes for their children.

(909) 621-6184

TOUGH LOVE, for providing support and guidance for families in trouble, emphasizing problem solving and children growing into responsible adults.

(215) 348-7090

AL ANON, for helping families recover from a family member's problem drinking.

(888) 4AL-ANON

CIRCLE OF PARENTS, for providing mutual-support groups in which parents can help each other.

(312) 663-3520

INDEX